T0171053

Recipes for..........
Self-healing

Recipes for..........
Self-healing

ELKE BULL

BALBOA.
PRESS
A DIVISION OF HAY HOUSE

Copyright © 2013 Elke Bull

All rights reserved. No part of this book may be used or reproduced by any means, graphic, electronic, or mechanical, including photocopying, recording, taping or by any information storage retrieval system without the written permission of the publisher except in the case of brief quotations embodied in critical articles and reviews.

Balboa Press books may be ordered through booksellers or by contacting:

Balboa Press
A Division of Hay House
1663 Liberty Drive
Bloomington, IN 47403
www.balboapress.com
1-(877) 407-4847

ISBN: 978-1-4525-7791-3 (sc)
ISBN: 978-1-4525-7790-6 (hc)
ISBN: 978-1-4525-7792-0 (e)

Library of Congress Control Number: 2013912459

Because of the dynamic nature of the Internet, any web addresses or links contained in this book may have changed since publication and may no longer be valid. The views expressed in this work are solely those of the author and do not necessarily reflect the views of the publisher, and the publisher hereby disclaims any responsibility for them.

The author of this book does not dispense medical advice or prescribe the use of any technique as a form of treatment for physical, emotional, or medical problems without the advice of a physician, either directly or indirectly. The intent of the author is only to offer information of a general nature to help you in your quest for emotional and spiritual well-being. In the event you use any of the information in this book for yourself, which is your constitutional right, the author and the publisher assume no responsibility for your actions.

Any people depicted in stock imagery provided by Thinkstock are models, and such images are being used for illustrative purposes only.
Certain stock imagery © Thinkstock.

Printed in the United States of America

Balboa Press rev. date: 07/26/2013

Contents

Introduction - The Concept of Self Healing vii

Part 1 - THE FACTS or Learning the basic principles 1

   1. No Matter the Prognosis or Disease 3
   2. The Body has a Natural Healing System 9
   3. Understanding Illness 11
   4. Taking Responsibility 15
   5. Mastering Energy 19
   6. The Mind Controls the Body 27
   7. Using the Holistic Approach 37
   8. Your Environment 41

Part 2 - Recipes to Heal Yourself 47

   1. Using the Energy Balance 55
   2. Focusing 59
   3. Love 63
   4. Affirmations 67
   5. Your Personal Environment 73
   6. Looking after Yourself & Your Body 81
   7. Tapping into the Source 95
   8. Creative Visualisation 105
   9. Mastery over Mind 117
  10. Attitude and Beliefs 131

11. Acceptance 137
12. Forgiveness...139
13. Prayer 153
14. Faith..157
15. Learning to Die..163
16. Learning to Live...169

Part 3 - The Ultimate Recipe 177

Part 4 - PUTTING IT ALL TOGETHER—You personal recipe..................187

Conclusion 197
List of Recipes.. 199
List of Diagrams..203
Bibliography.. 205
Index 209

Introduction

Inside you; inside every person is a special spark of energy that defines them. This spark makes their whole life possible. It is life itself and defines the possibilities you can achieve, who you are and will be within the limits of your ideas and choices. It holds the key to your health, wealth and happiness.

I am a healer and I heal individuals by leading them to the point where they can heal themselves. I teach the recipes for you to change your life. There is an old saying—Give a hungry man a fish and feed him for a day: teach him how to fish and feed him for a life-time. In this spirit I teach healing!

I know that within each of us is a healer—a magician that only needs awakening. It is within the reach of almost all people to regain our good health when we have become sick and maintain it—once we know how. While this text seems to primarily focus on healing as it pertains to health, the methods can just as easily be adapted to curing a sick income stream, visualising a new career path or attaining any life-goals so let us start with recipes for self-healing.

Let's establish that modern medicine is terrific and certainly has its place in the process of health and healing. Doctors have learnt to build new skin, replace hearts, and extend humanity's life span by decades. They have eliminated and can cure many diseases. This is not ground breaking news but simple fact. However, there is also a world of natural medicines and healing modalities and techniques. In some terminal cases there is nothing left to offer hope but alternative or miracle cures. Finally, when the time comes to pass over and leave this planet, there is a special need for a healing presence to move peacefully through the veil of death.

Practicing self-healing techniques can give each individual an active role to play, whatever the circumstances. It is something we can do for ourselves and for loved ones. Taking responsibility for our own wellness is the first step to helping and healing ourselves. Taking responsibility makes individuals feel more positive and connects to the soul within, reaching for hope and recovery by also accessing personal power.

As you get familiar with the ideas and techniques—the recipes for self-healing presented in this book, you will awaken the healer within you and come to realise that you too have the power to help yourself.

Many people use these techniques and are successful on various levels. Every little bit helps!

Let me demonstrate what I do. It is like baking a cake—you follow a recipe . . . .

The recipe I follow is simple:-

First—I see a medical practitioner and check the diagnosis. A correct diagnosis is vital to know what I am fighting.

Then—I ask lots of questions and discuss my medical options. This may include prescriptions for medication or medical procedures. I always take the prescriptions home with me.

Finally—When I get home I go to a quiet place and meditate on my own battle plan.

My battle plan includes the self-healing techniques you will learn about in this book. They mostly work along with my doctor's advice for a speedy recovery but I have sometimes deviated slightly from the recommendation. With this combination I have overcome problems that were according to medical opinion, expected to continue for the remainder of my life.

I use meditation, visualisations and mental focus, relaxation, reflexology, massage and channelled energy. I have used acupuncture to clear blocks and homeopathy for natural drops to balance my body, plus for the past 10 years I have been regularly using vibrational, therapeutic grade essential oils. These recipes keep me healthier, boost my immune system and keep me going when others get sick. When others catch "the flu" I stay healthy occasionally suffering a few short symptoms but recover quickly. Although I have noticed that I can withstand high levels of stress, when it persists and I forget to apply my techniques, I do become run-down just like anyone else. Then I find myself wondering at my lack of intelligence when I realise I could have been helping myself instead of coughing and sneezing and just expecting it all to go away. My father just laughs and reminds me I am human . . .

Good health practices and sensible lifestyle choices can generally maintain the body's natural healing process. Some of these practices are basic. A sensible diet, avoiding harmful excesses, regular exercise, adequate sleep and rest are vital to good health. These simple measures are especially important when fighting a health challenge and while combating or experiencing stress.

Making good lifestyle choices is the first of many simple ways of accessing your personal power and taking responsibility for yourself. Ever increasing numbers of people recognise the value of a healthy lifestyle and follow the convention that prevention is better than cure. That power of choice is a basic human right available to everyone but often forgotten and certainly under-rated.

Accepting responsibility for yourself and accessing your personal power often starts a chain reaction. The process begins with taking better care of yourself, and tuning into your own healing energies. After that you will also develop understanding on other levels. Then there is also a natural migration from helping ourselves, to helping loved ones and finally to healing planet earth. With success comes confidence. Exercising your personal power will give you an awesome feeling of reward, purpose and joy.

PLEASE NOTE that I am NOT a medical doctor and do NOT give medical advice. I teach techniques that can help people to help themselves and work with their doctor's treatment.

Any reader who is ill is encouraged to seek professional medical advice.

Australians are free to change doctors and to get a second or third opinion if they chose. Seeking professional medical advice is important and makes sense! If your car is not running efficiently you take it to a mechanic and a trained expert repairs it. Your body must be worthy of the same level of care and respect. A car is replaceable.

You only have one life. You only have one body to risk in any lifetime. Common sense would assume we all realise that serious conditions need more urgent help and any illness that has the potential to be life-threatening must be given special attention. This does not mean the process cannot be aided with self-healing techniques such as relaxation and meditation, prayer, affirmations, lying on of hands, moving energy and possibly the use of other modalities.

I fully recommend that if you are on medication—that you please continue that medication. I also recommend discussing any change in treatment with your prescribing medical practitioner. The techniques I describe in this book DO NOT replace or deny the benefits of conventional medication and medical procedures. They simply let you help yourself, initiate your responsibility for your own wellness and help activate and stimulate your inner natural healing mechanism.

Self-healing is a holistic means of helping current conventional treatment. Thinking positive cannot replace vital medication or operations. A broken leg needs to be correctly set by a doctor. Meditating will not align the bones but it will help them heal—knitting faster and stronger once the limb is set.

The steps for taking personal responsibility for your state of health or your recovery from illness or disease are simple. First use common sense. Then tune into your body. Finally take the action steps to look after it, pamper it when it wants attention and by all means have fun. Self-healing is powerfully transforming.

Take the time to learn some of the facts . . .

PART ONE

THE FACTS or Learning the basic principles

CHAPTER 1

No Matter the Prognosis or Disease . . .

It is a fact that—no matter which disease you choose or what the medical experts predict—some people will survive beyond expectations. We have all heard of stories of patients who were only expected to survive for months but go on living far beyond—still happy and healthy many years later. We have all heard of miracles. Study the particular cases and you will find varying magic ingredients or reasons for the survival. Talk to the people and they all have a story. I personally know of individuals who were apparently beyond medicinal help with their inoperable tumours and their only options were to have their names put on church prayer lists. Results varied from letting go of fear and dying peacefully to complete recovery. Two miracle recoveries stick in my mind. One changed his two months life expectancy into seven years. Another's tumour disappeared over a period of two years totally baffling doctors. Many such outcomes are documented.

The fact is that no matter the prognosis—some people will defy the odds and survive.

The passion for finding how this is possible has kept me delving into how these miracles happened, trying to discover how these people cured themselves and survived Perhaps we could copy the recipe for healing and extending life.

Imagine being able to create a miracle whenever you need it? Imagine knowing how to change outcomes, applying those techniques and healing yourself and others if the need arose.

What if you could learn these healing secrets to not only survive serious illness and regain your health when some serious problem manifested but you could retain perfect health and prevent future problems and challenges that might arise?

What if some magic healing secret could be uncovered, I wondered. I thought if there is a secret recipe that works and if only one additional person was healed who would have otherwise died . . . If even one person's suffering was able to be reduced . . .

Let us put the idea into statistical perspective. Imagine that some particular condition has a survival rate of 75%. That would mean that medication or conventional treatment could not cure twenty-five out of every hundred patients. If you were one of the seventy-five that lived, you would be happy. Problem solved for you.

Now let us SUPPOSE you had been one of the other twenty-five who would not survive. You would experience a totally different set of emotions. Instead of relief you could feel panic, anger, fear or any of a range of other negative emotions.

Now imagine accessing this recipe for self-healing. Imagine the effect that using some special techniques or recipe—perhaps even something I describe in this book having a healing effect that changed your results. Merely reading this book might open up your mind to the possibility of getting better and surviving, enough positive energy to let belief lead you to a set of circumstances that promote a positive outcome. That instance of changing your mind from focusing on death to considering life, may be enough to open the door to the precise actions to help you to change your life and create a new future. Suddenly you see the possibility of another chance at life.

Suppose you could make the 75% statistic into 76% by your survival. Would that not make a world of difference for you? And it would also improve the statistics which may give just a little more hope to someone else. It may even start a chain reaction.

People are individuals—each is different and unique. Each person has their own set of desires, goals and dreams and a level of intention to put them into action and make them manifest.

On a very basic level people have a desire or inner drive to live. That will to live is one vital ingredient called on in self-healing. That desire, intention or will is only one explanation of possible different outcomes between two people with almost identical problems. Doctors and nursing staff will often know immediately and intuitively which of two particular patients will recover by recognising a strong will to live. I recall reading one amazing case about this phenomenon. A widow was told at the birth of her child that she should arrange for its care. During the delivery process, it was discovered that she had cancer. Best prognosis at the time with all conventional treatment could let her live a maximum of 5 years. As the child's father was already dead, she felt it was her duty to raise their son. She considered her job would be finished when he had gone through college so she fought her disease. She extended her life from 5 years at best by almost five times. Only months before he graduated from medical school she finally lost her battle. This woman had literally willed herself to live twenty years past her original prediction. During this time she had a number of operations and constant medical and other treatments but she did succeed in her own healing journey and extended her life to the limit set in her mind.

Predictions are such dangerous things. They can severely hamper the inner healing process and limit life. Many people accept the time-span given to them by experts and then find that this limit becomes a self-fulfilling prophecy. When AIDS first became a recognized disease, statistics were released which stated most people lived from six months to two years after contracting the disease.

Patients believed the time limit and I wonder how many died needlessly early because they did not know that AIDS patients can survive for many years. Once we tell ourselves we have a limit to our life span, our body and mind can make this come true—that becomes a self-fulfilling prophecy.

To appreciate the workings of a Self-fulfilling prophecy, let me relate Crystal's story.

This is one real life example from my mother's circle of friends. Crystal was lovely She was a normal happy 50years old and quite suddenly she declared one night that she felt her life had been good. She mentioned she was now almost the same age as her mother when she died. Crystal confessed to her friends that she was still looking forward to enjoying another year or two with them before she expected to pass on.

Although perfectly healthy, Crystal carried within her mind a particular life expectancy. Mentally she set her time-clock. She carried a deep belief that she was near the end of her allotted time based on her mother's history.

She suddenly chose to move back to her birthplace in Europe. Shortly after arriving she had horrific chest and back pains. The doctor who came on the house-call checked her out and established nothing was wrong. She diagnosed a stress attack. Crystal passed away a few nights later in her lounge chair of a massive heart attack. She was aged 53. Outliving her mother by a little more than 2 years, Crystal coincidentally reached her own "used by" date.

There is another interesting story on setting mental time-limits. My friend, a doctor by profession, was very ill so she saw a specialist for his opinion and advice. Her colleague mentioned that she could reasonable expect to still enjoy another two years. He always gave all his patients his considered opinion and a time-limit believing they could then prepare themselves for the inevitable.

My friend may have had a rare and fatal lung condition but she also had a quick mind. Her reaction was quite radical. She was a devout lady who believed only God knew when her last moment would be. Her exact words were, "How can you presume to know when I will die? I might walk down the stairs, out the door and be run over by a bus. Where are my two years then?"

That statement shocked him into realizing how silly it is to guess. Healthy people may die and sick people may not. There are often surprises and it certainly makes no sense to be pessimistic or in setting up limiting expectations in the mind.

I will always remember the ten years I spent living in a small country town. On arrival, I was given the local tour and we passed a house in the neighbourhood. The owner lay dying in the local hospital. He had been very sick for a number of years and everyone in the district knew he didn't have long to go. On the next hill was a house with three teenage sons riding happily on motorbikes. They were sensible, knew how to handle machinery and you would assume, had long lives in front of them. Two years later one of those boys was killed in a horrific car smash. Not his fault but he still died instantly. The accident shocked the whole district. That old man was still "dying" when we left the town ten years later. I guess no-one told him how sick they thought he was. It brought home the fact to me that there is no guarantee in life except death. No matter what we might assume, things happen. People are born, they live, they die and pinpointing that timing is a somewhat nebulous matter.

CHAPTER 2

The Body has a Natural Healing System

The natural state for our body is abundant health. Almost all babies are born bouncing with health and grow—sometimes even despite what their parents do. It is only natural—just as the body should naturally be in a state of ease. Notice the words—This is how it should be. Illness is the state of dis-ease.

Our body is continually regenerating itself. We replace a whole layer of skin several times per year and almost every cell within our whole body, bones included at least once every single year. This continual regeneration process goes on throughout our whole lives and is constantly replacing our old worn-out cells with new ones.

Within our wonderful body, we also have an in-built defence system— our immune system. We have an in-built pharmacy and database of our medical history. When we are stressed, our bodies inject adrenaline into our blood stream to help us run away. When we are sad and cry our body releases calming and soothing substances that let us feel better. This is our own in-built medicine cabinet and should be always available to every one of us.

When we cut ourselves or skin our knee, the body instantly sends down glue-like cells that plug the hole. In time the skin heals. Under the scab and the body completely repairs itself without even a conscious thought. This is our natural healing system at work.

The subconscious mind behind our automatic healing system is very powerful and manifests in wonderful yet sometimes in strange ways. If we cannot tolerate something, we have an allergic reaction and the body will remember. Every time we go near that same condition, circumstances or substance we will get sick, as the body will remember its inability to cope. In some cases, this information of past trauma is so strongly deeply implanted within the mind that it limits normal life. One such problem is the inability to cope with confined spaces: another is the inability to cope with open spaces. However, once the mind is taught to overcome the initial trauma and fear, that particular problem can be overcome and the patient is cured.

Nevertheless, abundant health is the natural state and the body has a natural healing mechanism. Consider the instance of a broken arm or leg. First a doctor sets the limb back straight but the body itself knits the bone together. This healing process occurs quite naturally because the body repairs itself and heals itself automatically. The interesting fact is that this process will go faster or slower according to thought patterns of the individual and how much they are willing to help the process. Sleep and rest are often good medicine to let the body draw on natural energy to repair. Excessive activity will deplete reserves but movement is important to clear impurities and toxins from the body. At times it is a balance of opposites. Recognising the power of the body's natural healing mechanism is the first step to self-healing and tuning in to it is the next.

CHAPTER 3

Understanding Illness

I believe dis-ease and illness manifest in our lives for a variety of causes. At times quite by accident and at other times we draw them in for emotional or spiritual reasons—mostly quite unconsciously.

Let's look at some of the reasons.

- Illness and injury happens at random. We may just do something wrong—either by mistake or through carelessness. This accounts for accidents. Car accidents can kill people, can injure them permanently or leave them completely unharmed and wiser for the experience.
- Illness and injury results from proven physical causes such as poisons, viruses, bacterial infections . . . We are not happy with some aspect of life and we wish to escape. This accounts for our need for over-indulgence and abuse of our bodies. Whether we eat too much fat, we smoke too many cigarettes or eat food that contains too much sugar, salt, or other additives to enhance flavour, we will get sick. When we are stressed for an extended period, we get stomach ulcers and heart disease. Our bodies are not built to withstand prolonged pressure beyond some

particular intangible point so we get ill and escape temporarily or we die and escape permanently.

- Illness and compromised health comes as a spiritual lesson. We get ill because we need to learn something. When my father had his heart attack, our whole family learnt a huge number of things. We were all reminded how fragile our bodies can be and that we need to take care of them. We came to realise how most of us take good health and each other for granted. We discovered how much work he did in our family business that the rest of us did not know how to do. He on the other hand learnt to slow down, stop focusing only on his work and look after his body and himself first for a change. He came to realise that no matter how important it is to look after business, his health, and life are ultimately more important.

- Emotional needs manifest illness and health challenges. We get ill because we want attention. As a child, we are taught by the example of family that the sick are special and are pampered. Children grow into adults but their mind does not flick a switch and say NOW you are grown up and what worked for you as a child is no longer valid. Adults need love, they need attention, and the knowledge that they are special to someone just as the sick child did years ago. At times we get sick, to let our own sub-conscious mind and those around us remind us that we are special. We get a headache or minor virus to encourage family and friends show their concern. We get attention, our need is filled, and we get better. I know of one woman who had 20 years of minor procedures and operations until her husband finally came to the conclusion that she is only happy when she is sick and being pampered. She did her duty while she was well but looking after her family took on the feeling of greatness and sacrifice while during the times she was 'ill'. It made her feel like she was heroic to work despite her illness—a huge effort just to look after her family. As a reward, she felt that she deserved lavish attention. Her illness was real and no doubt so was her pain. Sometimes I have wondered how much of her pain she caused herself through this need to play out the martyr role of life.

- Illness can be the way to passing on. Finally, we can use an illness to move on. When we are ready to leave this life, we can do it in two ways. We can leave suddenly—by being fatally injured or being in some major accident or incident. Or we can move on slowly by lingering illness or disease. Old age is the disease of having used the body to its physical use-by date. And so we get ill or pass away in our sleep. This process seems to me to be peaceful and natural.

- The placebo effect is invaluable with "imagined" conditions. Some diseases are only in the mind but they can feel painful and real to the sufferer. We often attract these diseases without knowing that we are doing it. When I was a child, my mother worked in a large factory that employed thousands of women. She had a minor yet very painful accident and the on-site nurse unlocked the medicine chest to give her painkillers. My mother was curious why she was not given some from the large jar marked painkillers on the front desk. The nurse explained about the concept of placebos. The so-called 'painkillers' contained nothing more than glucose and yet a large numbers of women needed their daily supply to rid them of the headaches they got from travel and work. Their pain was real and the tablets they thought were pain suppressors 'cured' that real pain through the power of their minds.

The placebo effect is often misunderstood and not utilised to its true potential. It accesses the body's intrinsic healing mechanism and the power of the mind does the rest. Symptoms disappear.

How often has a Band-Aid cured the pain of the scraped knee? I can recall taking my then three-year-old to the doctor with pain in the stomach. The doctor enquired about the Band-Aid across the little tummy. I explained it made little pains go away. He smiled and said he wished more mothers used that idea to gauge whether a child had a real pain that demanded medical attention or just wanted to be pampered. We were living in the country and each trip to the doctor took a long time. I did not want to make unnecessary trips. I did not want to be branded a hypochondriac mother but at the same time no mother wants to be unfair and watch her child to suffer. The Band-Aid trick made sure that all legitimate problems were still treated promptly without wasting time on false alarms.

Being open-minded is important and healthy. Being consciously aware that there are benefits to illness, such as gaining attention, open the mind to a new way of thinking. We begin to see why other people may choose to get ill, and can transfer that to ourselves. Is the migraine today only to avoid going shopping with aunty? Or is it real and something to get checked out?

Once we accept that illness is not the natural state for human bodies, we get motivated and active in claiming back our birthright of abundant health. When we find the source of our own illness and get it diagnosed correctly, we can begin to fight it. That is the point of personal power. We can release or let go of our need for the diseases and get back to enjoying living life.

Sometimes there is no identifiable reason for a person's lack of thriving health. Sometimes people get ill because they do. It just happens and we cannot find any particular reason. That does not mean there is nothing to learn from the experience. It does not negate any personal development of an individual taking more care of their body, changing to a healthy life-style or exploring possible procedures and cures.

Whatever the reason for the illness or disease, whatever time in life, the state of one's health needs to be accepted and actioned. If symptoms persist, it is important to look forwards with optimism towards effecting an improvement or cure rather than backwards focusing on a possibly illusive cause. Often it is not as important how, why or what caused the problem as time invested to focus on improving or regaining health. The past is dead and gone. It cannot be changed. Now is the point of power. Now creates the future. The ideas and actions of today literally manifest tomorrow.

CHAPTER 4

Taking Responsibility

We live in a new age of learning and knowledge and this puts power in the hands of each individual. We have choices but also responsibility.

In personal health and well-being, there has been a subtle shift in responsibility. Last century, in the past few generations, once someone was sick they went to a doctor. The doctor was responsible for a cure. S/he would decide what we had and would then treat the problem with medicine or an operation.

Today people often explore alternative treatments to clear aliments and health challenges themselves. That means they are actually taking responsibility for themselves. In most cases that is good but occasionally if they are not following good advice they may be taking their lives into their own hands in the process.

Mothers have home-births, and are fine in normal circumstances. I personally did not have the courage to do that and preferred the safety of having my children in a hospital. Knowing everything was on hand in case of emergency, in case a problem was to occur gave both my doctor and especially me, a sense of security.

I take responsibility for me by taking an active role, asking a lot of questions during my consultation with my doctor. I have been taking prescription medicine to control my blood pressure for some time now. As the blood pressure has now reduced, it is still being monitored by my doctor until he is satisfied that I am OK to be without medication. It all depends on the seriousness and severity of the symptoms. I always err on the side of caution and have become very intuitive in knowing when to go for help. Stress is easily alleviated with a bath in essential oils but for prolonged agitation there may be a more sinister cause. Only a medical practitioner can diagnose illness or prescribe treatment. Taking responsibility for oneself means calling in specialists when necessary. Meditation cannot cure a heart attack.

I also concentrate on prevention, knowing that it is often easier to prevent an illness than it is to cure one. Living a healthy life-style is very important. Getting adequate rest and relaxation during times of stress is vital.

As long as thousands of years ago, people used medicine men and healers who relied on herbs, spices and oils to help us get over our problems. Some of these natural medicines have since been investigated by chemical companies who research them, develop medicines from their active ingredients and patent commercial drugs. Are we circling back to this place of taking responsibility of our own health? When we go to medical professionals to help us and assume a spirit of partnership, we are being responsible for ourselves. We stand in our own power rather than being a victim looking for a saviour.

Medical procedures today are almost daily miracles. Incredible operations and procedures can repair so much. There are often several options but sometimes this makes it harder to make informed choices. Taking responsibility is sometimes hard.

Being in control is about choice. It is also diagnosis and prognosis. For these a qualified health professional is advisable. Perhaps some tests are recommended to find the cause. Control and self-reliance is not a matter of staying away from doctors but in working as a team. It is recognising who the experts are and balancing the choice. Depending on the health challenge the risks of a wrong choice may be small or fatal. For this reason, I always recommend to err on the side of caution and get the opinion of the expert in the field.

I take responsibility for my health with calculated risk. I begin by checking it out early. Taking responsibility for my own health does not mean I avoid doctors or other health professionals. With professional diagnosis, I explore any alternatives and use whatever I feel is right for me.

Here is a personal example of the process I follow. Early in my self-healing journey, I got severe pains in my right hip that I overcame completely with affirmations. When the pains stopped I thought the problem was cleared but six months later the pains came back. This time I noticed that the pains coincided with menstruation. They were more severe. I know pain is nature's warning and by returning I knew that there was a problem. I saw my doctor.

He sent me for a number of tests to check out all the nasty possibilities. The tests he made fortunately came back negative. His conclusion was the hip pain was reflected from my ovaries and the problem was actually hormonal. His forecast was that I would experience this pain until menopause. He was reluctant to cut away healthy organs, so medically he did nothing more. I was totally happy with this idea.

My biggest triumph was I now I knew what I was fighting. I went home and put together a battle plan. The first were hands on healing and mind techniques like dynamic visualisations and affirmation. There was a steady improvement and the condition cleared. I felt a definite success in this healing business! But . . .

A bit over a year later it came back again. The thought of enduring until menopause—my doctor's suggestion—still did not appeal to me. During my next meditation I asked for an answer. By complete chance I was led to a homeopath who gave me a clear bottle of hormone drops.

I took the drops and went back to my visualisations and affirmations. Everything cleared again over the next two months and it hasn't come back in the 15 years that have passed since.

The experience opened my mind to homeopathy and expanded my knowledge and my options. I worked with health professionals utilising their expertise but on my terms and for a great outcome.

CHAPTER 5

Mastering Energy

Understanding energy is the most important part of any healing.

There is an energy, which is in and passes through everything. This universal energy is also known as the life-force. It exists in everything. It is in each animal, plant—even in rocks. I guess this give new meaning to the concept of a pet rock.

Energy vibrates in a low but measurable electromagnetic frequency. There is a scale of vibration levels. Animals have higher frequency than plants but a lowed vibration than humans.

The human energy field has been photographed with fascinating results. Kirilian photography, named after the scientist who first developed the method, not only proves the existence of the life-force but energy centres within the body. Ancient religions and cultures have believed in the concept of life-force energy and psychics have seen it since the beginning of time. It is believed that we all used to be able to tune in to and see these energies clearly but have lost the skill.

The significance of energy is basically easy to understand. Life is vibrant energy. Death is the absence of this moving energy. Illness is a stage of waning energy. Awareness of energy levels and just understanding the concept of life-force energy explains how natural healing modalities work.

Some people—psychics, meditating monks and children, just to group them in a few categories, often see these energies as colours. Most adult western people cannot see them but many feel them. On a subconscious level we also see and sense them.

Awareness of life-force energy and vibrations may sound unscientific and in the realm of hippies and voodoo but can be measured and photographed. Understanding energy, seeing and feeling it, actually has many simple but powerful applications to health and wellness. Once you understand energy and use the ideas, you will have the power to improve many areas of your life. If you read this book with an open mind focusing only to improve your personal vibration, you will achieve miracles in your life.

The mind is the single most powerful mechanism that affects personal vibrational energy. All thoughts have a measurable frequency and create a vibration in the body. Take a moment to think of something you fear and then concentrate on the feeling you have in your body. Does your stomach knot up? Are you colder? Is your heart racing? Now take a moment to think of someone you love or imagine your dream coming true. Perhaps you can imagine winning a new car? Do you feel like you are lighter? Has your heart opened up? Do you have a smile on your face? High vibrations feel good.

Low vibrations feel bad. The important fact to note is that vibrations can be triggered in the body from thoughts held in the mind. What and how you think can affect your body. It is can all be explained on a level of vibrations and energy and has a profound effect on health.

I find it interesting that this concept of maintaining health through vibrations has been taught by religions through the ages but referred to as the battle between "good and evil".

Let's take a little journey and explore the concept of good and evil as a line or an energy continuum. Notice that evil is live spelt backwards and they are at opposite ends of the scale. It is like they are at the opposite end of a line.

evil------------------good.

Everything that has two ends also has a middle. The middle is the point of balance and the point of power. Imagine the line of energy representing life in general. If we take the aspect of time into consideration then the point of power is NOW and the middle. Considering time as energy— one side of NOW is the past and the other is the future. We expect to have a future to live but our past is consumed and gone so it is the opposite of live and becomes "evil".

------past------NOW------future------

The future contains hope and hope is full of possibility and opportunity to live. This can easily be classed as good. The past has no hope because it has already happened. It is not bad as an opposite of good but it no longer carries any opportunity. We have the power to affect our future but we cannot change our past. The only power we have over the past is in reflection: we can change how we think and feel about our past.

When we have something we look forward to, then we want to go forward into the situation and feel good in anticipation of it. If we like going to the beach or the opera, we happily look forward expecting good. When we know we have to do something unpleasant, we become reluctant to move. The most unpleasant emotion of fear can cause us to delay or totally freeze up to paralysis. When I have something I consider is bad I always carry a secret wish to have it behind me—in my past. This is the motivator for me to take action towards any challenging fear I have to overcome. Imagine a visit to the dentist or fronting up to the boss when we have to admit we have just made a BIG mistake—perhaps one that will cost a lot of money to repair. We can change the lables on the energy continuum and class the feelings as . . .

------negative------NOW------positive------

Life is like this on a huge scale. If we have lots of good things happening we think our life is good. When a number of things occur that we think are bad we judge our life as bad. We balance it all up without understanding what we can do about it. We live life without realising or using our personal power to create the future rather than react to the present as a consequence of the past.

Understanding energy helps in realising the consequences of thoughts and feelings to outcomes—experiences and situations are our life. Every individual has some control over their power of thought and choices made are the power over life in general. This is the power and knowledge to use to full advantage and improve health of body, wealth of experience and happiness of life in general.

Let us look at the positive aspect. Have you noticed that you get excited when you can do something you like to do? Watch children playing and see the excitement explode if you promise to take them somewhere special. They jump for joy. This is increased energy. It comes from anticipation of good, hope of fun to come, and being happy. This energy is beneficial to health. Do we not visit sick friends to cheer them up?

Now let us look at the other side or the negative. When we are ill or depressed, do we feel like dancing or jump for joy? Of course not! Illness robs us of our energy. We do not feel like doing anything when we are depressed and our spirits are low.

We can now draw our energy line. LOW on the left and HIGH on the right of the central point.

It is simply a matter of different words for the same energy. Write these ideas below one another and notice they all match somewhat. The past is dead and we cannot change it only view the fact differently. Those who are ill feel down or low, unhappy and generally do not want to do much or get involved in life. All these are rather negative.

The other side of the centre looks more positive. People in a happy mood, people who are vibrantly healthy are generally also optimistic. Their future looks brighter and they have more things to be happy about. There is joy in life and hope in the future. But real life is not strictly black and white because life unfolds on many levels simultaneously.

Life is very simple but can appear to be so very complex because so many things are happening to us at the same time. We may be happy because we have just heard good news from a friend, upset because the milk we wanted for our tea or coffee is sour and hope we get the promotion at work all at the same time. At any given moment, we may be on the side of low energy for a number of situations and the high energy for some others. How we feel in ourselves is a balance of the two.

These different variables are also weighted depending on our values and beliefs. Unfortunately the simple idea becomes complicated.

One issue may seem quite minor while another devastating. Sour milk and no more chocolate biscuits in the tin cannot bring us down if we have just won $500 in a raffle. Getting a promotion may suddenly be meaningless if your child is in hospital with a serious illness. The amount of positive or negative energy given to each incident depends on how important the outcome of an issue is. Let me explain here that negative energy is low energy because it is a actually a lack of energy. When we are stressed out, we feel that we are drained and that is exactly right. We have no energy left and our stress has left us feeling empty.

Understanding our personal energy is important for an understanding the mystery of healing and how it actually works. The two disciplines of acupuncture and acupressure heal by stimulating the body's natural energy releasers. Psychic and spiritual healers channel healing energies into their patients as their way of helping the receiver's healing process. They often work in terms of light seeing illness in terms of darkness or areas of the body lacking energy. These are a couple of ways of working with energy, different ways of applying healing modalities.

As this is a difficult concept, I will explain with a story.

My friend Mary, had a pain in her side and visited a clairvoyant healer who gave her comfort, energy, and counselling. He explained to her the need to seek medical attention and of checking into serious pain. She was very reluctant but he persisted and finally convinced her to make an appointment "just to eliminate any possible nasties". The psychic had picked up that the woman had cancer in the colon and liver and would probably not survive six months in her current condition. When this healer touched the patient, he saw her body as light and the areas of illness as black surrounded by a bright red line. The feeling he got from her was fear, sadness, and desperation. He saw a picture of her coffin and the words Easter in light beyond this to the right and in the future. The outcome of predictions such as this can sometimes be changed with quick powerful actions and strong mental beliefs. The only help he could give this lady at the time was to encourage her to seek immediate medical advice in the hope that this may cure her and to continually channel the necessary energy to give her the courage and strength to take her life one step at a time. Her doctor saw her next day and admitted her quickly into hospital. Test revealed secondary cancer in the liver and primary in the colon. She had operations and treatments. She also had a rigid and unsupportive belief system. Mary knew in her heart of hearts that everyone who had "bad cancer" as she termed her condition died within a couple of months of being diagnosed. Deep within her she always knew that she would find the man of her dreams just before she died. She had recently met a wonderful man she had fallen in love with. In her mind it was all falling into place and consequently she died a week before Easter.

There is a place for each type of healer and each treats according to how they interpret the energy. The surgeon sees the physical body and removes the cancer while the psychic healer sees the lack of light and warmth and channels energy. Together they confirm the relationship between sickness and lack of light or energy. So how does this help us?

The energy continuum has at the centre the point of balance. Image this imaginary line and you can begin to help in your own healing process. Situations, experiences, and people can be somehow pegged on this line in terms of energy. The effect they have on you can be classified as either those who enhance or build energy versus those who deplete you and your energy.

Generally we are all happy to be around people we like. They are the people who make us feel better when we are ill or depressed. They will cheer us up or raise our energies. Everyone also knows other people who have the reverse effect. They are draining. Everyone knows at least one. This is the kind of person who visits you in hospital, finds out what you have wrong with you and then tells you of all the people he/she knows who died or were totally debilitated by your type of problem. This is the kind of cheering up anyone can do without but it is especially harming while you are ill because it will drain you further. It is best to tell them you are busy or tired and avoid contact.

Energy raisers and depleters come in all forms. They are not only in the form of people but are things, films, books, activities. It all depends completely on our individual choices. We are all different people and have different likes and dislikes. Basically, those things that make us happy will raise our energies, those we detest will lower them, and those that bore us do little either way.

Whether we are healthy and wish to continue to enjoy good health, whether we are ill and wish to get better or whether we just want more out of our lives, we MUST choose whatever makes the energy balance increase in our favour. When we begin moving with the natural flow of the universe from the positive side we are healing ourselves and our life improves. Be assured that everyone will make mistakes by making the wrong choice from time to time, but life is so full of so many little things that it is the overall balance which makes the difference.

CHAPTER 6

The Mind Controls the Body

Did you know that it is not what happens to us in this life that is important but how we feel and what we think about it. Let me explain what I mean with an example.

Imagine students having just finished their exams and receiving their grades. Some will fail and how they react will fall into two categories.

1. They may accept the situation. Perhaps he or she did their best and will sit again next year with better chance of passing. The other knows that he could have worked harder and actually deserved to fail for lack of performance.
2. Another person might not be able to accept the situation. Viewing this small failure as a fatal flaw, failure at life and consequently drops out of the whole course due to lack of confidence and underrating self.

Of those who passed, many would be relieved that they can keep going as expected. For them the pass is only confirmation of their self-evaluation. There will be some who wanted and got their top marks who are satisfied. In rare instances, a student who expected top but only reached second top commits suicide because they think they are failures.

All these different views of the outcomes depend on the attitude and belief each individual has about themselves. In fact, the standards we set for ourselves are only beliefs, success and failure are imaginary points we set according to these standards. Our life does not depend on these imaginary lines but we often act as though it did.

We set standards for every area of our life including our health. Some individuals expect people of 60 years of age to be old and frail while others know anyone 80-year-old and beyond can still be active. Whatever we believe, whatever standards we set in our minds become our benchmarks and put the boundary on our own possibilities. And attitudes can change over time. I remember Colin when he was thirty. He laughed about elderly people and he considered everyone as old and decrepit at age 65. Now it doesn't seem as funny to be old since his 60th birthday!

Our parents, our environment, and our experiences build our attitudes and beliefs. These attitudes and beliefs come in through thoughts we have and judgments we make. When we have heard or thought a particular idea often enough, we begin to believe it is true. The mind can be taught anything. I went to school with a girl whose brother had a type of colour blindness. He saw green as orange. It seemed strange to me at the time but what does it matter what name we give the colour of the leaves on the tree. For him the world looked normal with a green sunset and orange grass. No matter the colour, the grass was still there and so was the sunset. It was still beautiful. His mind only picked it up differently. In the same way we think thoughts, draw our conclusion, and then believe ideas that set an attitude. It is the attitude which determines how we how we feel about our life.

Let me repeat that it is not what happens as much as how we feel about what has happened that is important. Imagine a cat is run over on the road. You may feel sorry or not care at all about the incident. As soon as you find out it was your pet cat then your level of feeling changes immediately. It may be the same dead cat but how you feel about it changes dramatically. Our attitude predetermines our feelings and how we feel is how we think of life. If we feel happy, we think we are enjoying life. If we feel sad, we know we are having a rough trot. Our attitude to life is important in the concepts of health and self-healing. This is the power of the mind over the body. The winner's creed clearly explains this idea.

A WINNERS CREED

If you think you are beaten you are;
If you think you dare not, you don't;
If you'd like to win but think you can't'
Its almost a cinch you won't.
If you think you'll lose, you're lost,
For out in the world we find
Success begins with a person's will
Its all in the state of mind.
Life's battles don't always go
To the stronger or faster hand;
But sooner or later the person who wins
Is the one who thinks "I can".

Walter Wintle

Your mind-set or attitudes control your thinking and manifest in your state of health. I will always remember one particular seminar I attended in Brisbane. We had about 500 people in the room and were taught about the power of our attitude. At the time news headlines flashed that the US President had been shot at. Our teacher explained that he knew that the president would be fine and would recover quickly from his ordeal because of his belief system and attitude. Apparently in a previous interview, the president had told a news crew not to worry because he was a fast healer. This is a very positive and beneficial attitude to health.

Catching colds and viruses are much the same. I recall one man who had double pneumonia as a teenager and the "wise old doctor" predicted that this meant he had weak lungs and be very susceptible to colds for the rest of his life. This man developed chronic asthma at aged 35 and was the first person in every flu season to be sick and would generally have 2 bouts. Many years later this man learnt self-healing through mind-control and he changed his attitude towards good health. Telling his body that he had already endured more than enough colds for the rest of his life, he now goes through the whole flu season with no more than a day or two with a little sniffle. The sniffle does not last because he has statistically had his lifetime share of the flu. Having changed his attitude, has allowed him to regain his good health. It may sound like a small achievement but for him and his family, it has made a huge difference.

What detrimental attitudes could you eliminate to make your life easier? Think for a moment about any new beliefs which may smooth out your road?

Just as we consciously choose to like or dislike a piece of art or fashion or the food we prefer to eat, we can also choose to be healthy. It may take some time for us to build an attitude of good health. Our current state of health and age will have an effect on the speed of change but using mind over body makes it possible.

Consider for a moment that it takes as much effort to think, "I will heal quickly" as it does to think "Oh, Boy will I take ages to get over this." The important factor is that it is our choice what we think. Why not choose healthy beneficial thoughts?

Thoughts have power! No one has ever given up smoking by thinking and knowing that it was impossible to give up. Every person, who has kicked the habit has made a choice, believed that it was achievable and focused on others who have given up or on the idea of being a non-smoker themselves.

Without thinking so, it will not happen. Giving up smoking is not hard: some people have done it three times in one day! Knowing that you are a non-smoker today is much like drinkers who are non-drinking alcoholics. They give up for this day today and string one single day behind the other until they have succeeded for years. Their belief lets them give up for one day knowing that that is not such a huge task or a sacrifice. Then they keep tricking their mind that it is always that one day and it works. Huge tasks must be broken into manageable pieces.

Patients who are given notice they have a terminal illness can use this same technique of breaking down time. Changing time into two timeframes of today and afterwards, focuses the mind into the present. Over time, this can achieve wondrous things. In fact, we all have only this one moment of now to live in but without the threat of a terminal illness or chronic disease hanging over us we forget that life is terminal. We are all only here until we die. Being born we will all eventually die! We just do not think of it until someone tells us or reminds us. Maybe life would be more rewarding if we lived each day as if it our last.

> Note to self: Be more aware and accept
> that we only ever have today!

Acceptance of a condition is not the same as focusing on it. When my friend accepts that he is alcoholic and says he chooses not to drink today, he does not emotionalise this statement—just calmly states a fact. He has done this for the past eight years continuing to stay sober. If we have a terminal condition, accepting it does not mean we will not continue to enjoy the time we have left and/or fight to extend that time. It means the reverse.

We can accept the illness which exists at this point in time, but count it as though it does not by focusing on life. Acceptance is not giving in but controlling our own mind to focus away to a better place.

One of the most powerful weapons we have for controlling our mind is the power of the imagination. Unfortunately, we often let this work against us. How often have you had something go wrong, imagined it was life threatening and found it to be nothing. I had a little growth on my arm. At the time, I had spent many years working in the sun and each summer we endured a flood of media advertisements advising to check for possible skin cancers. My growth did not look like a cancer. It did not feel like a cancer, but I could not be 100% sure. My mind kept reminding me that my friend's mole was malignant. Graphically I remembered that she had a large part of her muscle removed because the cancer had spread. My mind would not leave me in peace and my imagination kept working to remind me of all the nasty possibilities. I finally went to my doctor. He removed a small area leaving me with a 1-centimetre scar. Tests revealed he had removed a wart but that doctor has the opinion that he would rather remove 100 unnecessary warts than leave one melanoma which could cost a patient's life. And what if that patient was you?

Our imaginations are very powerful instruments. Many times, we do not even realise we possess this power in our own minds yet anyone who has ever been to a movie should be able to relate quite easily. We watch actors on set stages on a screen and feel with them. In our imagination, we become the hero or the heroine. We feel their pain and anguish. We love, hate, and cry with them. We pay money for the privilege. The price of the ticket is for the experience of living a dream with the characters in our imagination. If you could imagine that we were a pirate, space-traveller or fighting a dragon then you can also imagine your health being perfect and free of illness.

You can take a holiday away from pain and distress and think of happy healing thoughts. When you are plagued by nightmares or your mind plays you horrible pictures in those small hours when the entire world is peacefully asleep, you can choose to think different thoughts. When all are asleep except those who are ill and suffering, except for the odd insomniac, you can use your imagination to program health and wellbeing. The idea might sound silly but like a computer can only run one program in the foreground, the mind can only think of one thing at a time. While you concentrate on having a holiday on the beaches of Hawaii or diving amongst the pretty coral on the Great Barrier Reef you cannot also draw your problems blacker than black unless you change your thought patterns. With a little practice, your imagination can return to that of your childhood—back to a time when you played out your dreams in happy hours of make-believe.

During this make-believe you know it is not real. Just like you know the movie is not real, but you can still be lost in the enjoyment of the moment. That is controlling your imagination instead of letting your imagination have the power over you. Eventually things never turn out quite as bad as we can imagine them to be, just as we do not eat a meal as hot as it is cooked.

At this point, it is important to explain a little about the mind.

Actually, we have two levels of mind. We have the conscious mind which lets us think and analyse, and we have a subconscious that contains our beliefs and attitudes. This is much like a computer. It holds a program for us to work with—the conscious mind. It also has a level of data where the actual program is written—the sub-conscious mind. This deeper mind cannot think and just accepts what it is told—just as we cannot change our game or program while we are using it.

We build our belief systems like we write a program. Let me explain. If we decide we want to create a cartoon, our conscious mind makes the decision. We collect our paper and pencil and begin to draw. It may be nowhere close to what we really wanted to draw and so we tell ourselves we are not good at sketching. When we try a second time and still do not improve we begin to have a belief about our inability to draw. We are unconsciously writing the program into our subconscious as we prove it to ourselves. Eventually, at some stage we hold that belief in our sub-conscious. We know we cannot draw or sketch. Unless we make a firm decision to learn this art, we will continue to be bad at drawing because we have set that barrier into our mind.

We hold barriers in many areas of our life. These barriers limit us in various ways including our thoughts about our health. As we set up belief systems in our sub-conscious, we can affect our own healing process. Beneficial knowledge can help our healing and destructive beliefs can keep any disease healthy. I know my body has a natural ability to heal itself and whenever I am sick I know it is only a temporary condition caused by something I am learning to overcome. I firmly believe that I recover quickly from any setbacks and have a high pain threshold. I use my common sense to realise that once I control my mind I also control my body and this works for me.

On the other hand, I also have a girl-friend, who has worked very hard in her life, and holds the belief that her body is worn out. This is not just an attitude but a deep-seated belief. She has numerous complaints and will regularly consult up to three different doctors for their opinions on her current pain and sickness. She gets the attention she is seeking while she suffers from every virus and illness that circulates among the population. Her state of health is consistent with the belief system that she has implanted into her sub-conscious.

What do you believe about yourself? Is it beneficial to abundant health or restrictive and helps draw illness towards you. Do you expect to be, become, and remain healthy?

The most incredibly helpful piece of information that anyone has ever discovered about the sub-conscious mind is that it cannot tell the difference between what is real and what is only imagined. Just as we enjoy the experiences at a movie and they seem real in our mind, so we can change or reprogram the data in our on-board computer.

As we change our minds and choose to believe new ideas, we set up new thought patterns. Be warned—This process of reprogramming the mind generally takes time!

We may have already told ourselves a thousand times that we cannot give up smoking. Just saying once or twice that we now believe a new idea about being a non-smoker, will not instantly erase the old belief. It takes persistence and a little dedication. It takes mental work of affirming the change, creatively visualizing the new self and strength to resist giving up this new belief before it has a change to become true. Good health is one of the most important things in this life and it deserves some effort. Using our mind to overcome any obstacles may seem challenging but it also makes life easier and more pleasant.

Our mind can be our best friend once we know some of the age-old secrets. Each of us not only has a conscious and a sub-conscious mind but also a link into the data-banks of the intelligence of the universe. Through our sub-conscious, we can link into a level of mind beyond ourselves. We do this quite naturally when we reach for ideas. Poets, artists, musicians, writers, scientists and inventors consistently plug into pure inspiration. They are not the only people who have this access. We all do.

Whenever we get a brilliant idea that we did not remember from previous experience; when we are creating or being inspired—we are tapping into this mind-source beyond our conscious selves.

We can reach this source of intelligence within ourselves for answers to our own health. This inner guidance system generally tells us when we have had enough to drink or when it is time for our next regular check-up. Suddenly we get the urge to eat oranges or stock up vitamin C and a day later someone at work comes in with a cold. When you begin to tune into this source of information you will often, quite coincidentally, do the right thing. I know there is no such thing as coincidence or accident because I have worked with my inner guidance for many years, in all areas of my life, not just related to health matters.

My life has been liberally sprinkled with difficulties. I am not always perfectly tuned in and sometimes make wrong choices. I suppose I am nevertheless still human! BUT I have learnt quite definitely, that when the little voice inside me gives advice and I do not listen, I meet with strife. My inner guidance system is my most trusted source of information.

CHAPTER 7

Using the Holistic Approach

Human beings exist on many levels. When we think of ourselves, generally we think first about our body. The body is the tangible part of us that we can see, feel, hear, smell, and touch. But there is more to us than a body. Much more.

Inside our skin somewhere intangible, is the spark of energy that gives us life. It is that special difference between our body being alive or dead. It is an elusive, invisible aspect that no surgeon has been able to touch. Some people call it our spirit and feel it is to our body like our mind is to our brain. Religions explain this in different words but it is actually more of the essence of what we call our true selves.

Deep within the solar plexus is a spot, seen as a spark of light by psychics. It is the very last place to loose body heat when we pass from this life. Maybe this is the place within us, just under our heart, deep within our breast, where we truly live. This is the centre of feeling, for this is the place that expands when we are proud and feels love when we are happy or moved. This is the place that feels tension when we are ill and heavy when we are depressed.

Spiritual healers often lay their hands on this spot on the centre of the chest and the top of the head of their clients. Perhaps this is because spiritual healing considers healing as more than just ridding the body of disease. True healing also incorporates the mind and the spirit. It looks at the individual as a whole person, being body, mind, and spirit. Each of these parts or aspects of us has it's place, roles to fulfil and needs. Our body needs food, water, and exercise to be vibrantly healthy and thrive. Our mind needs stimulation, but also quiet time to create and think. The mind works very well if it given time out. Some of us play chess, others do crossword puzzles or play computer games. People sit in nature, paint or do any of a thousand different activities to relax. Our spirit needs love, inner peace, and joy. For complete balance, we need to have all spheres in tune. These aspects of life also affect each other. If we eat the wrong foods or consume alcohol then both body AND mind works slower. When we are in love and feel great, we are happy and pains can disappear.

Problems overlap too. When we have financial problems we often get pain in the lower back, and everyone knows that stress will cause stomach ulcers among a myriad of health problems. Research has shown that stress can be traced back to being the onset of the majority of illness and particularly brings on the effects of aging.

Whenever I see a health problem, I always look deeper into the life of the ailing individual, me included. It is sometimes hard to tell another that their physical problem comes from the mental defect of negative thinking, harbouring resentment or focusing their thinking in a truly inappropriate direction. For example Craig—an over-weight young man I was working with, would only ever walk in little baby-steps when he had to go somewhere he was afraid of or do something he thought he didn't like, such as exercise. He coincidentally also had a huge self-image problem that stopped him walking boldly into life and claiming his good. Since he has lifted his self-image, he has lost weight. He now supplements his diet with vitamins, minerals, and trace elements. He takes the time to meditate and he walks for exercise. Self-image is closely related to self-respect. He now takes normal steps in his walking as he does in his life. I was fascinated that the two were so directly related. When we limit one aspect of ourselves, other parts of our life will also contract. This happens because each one of us is the centre of our own universe.

It seems that life is the glue that holds our minds and spirit into our body. Everything else radiates out from there much like a spider's web. No matter where you give it a little tug, it seems to affect all the rest in some way.

Life is really a miracle and although we have advanced far in science, life cannot be duplicated by man. The mystery of life remains the same miracle it was thousands of years ago. We may be able to take an egg and add some sperm in a petri dish but the miracle that combines the spirit/mind into the body is still special and as yet unable to be manufactured.

In a way we live two lives. We are in both this physical plane of matter and the mind/spirit plane of our psyche at the same time. We can be here and think about somewhere else at the same time. Perhaps we should expand our ideas of health and healing beyond the physical of operational procedures and chemical medicines and into holistic healing of considering our spirit/mind when we ill. Problems occur on multi-levels and so do the healing solutions to bring body/mind/spirit back into harmony and balance. Pain and illness are the physical manifestation of a problem. They are dis-ease in the body and merely the opposite to the natural state of health. Finding solutions and addressing causes is sometimes more than just alleviating the symptoms. Understanding the interconnectedness of our complex human being and using a holistic approach to finding a solution can bring true and lasting healing as opposed to just learning to cope with problems.

CHAPTER 8

Your Environment

As a complex human being we have an inner universe that affects our state of health. We are also affected by the outer universe, which I will call our environment. I suppose the easiest way of explaining the extent of our environment is to radiate out from our inner self. Consider your body. It breathes the air of the physical place in which you live. Be it town, country, or inner city. This is either fresh or polluted. Wherever it is, the air quality has an effect on your physical body. When rats were deprived of fresh air in lab experiments, it was scientifically proven that oxygen is linked to health and longevity.

The benefits of walking in the fresh air, as an aerobic exercise versus the harm pollution is really doing can be derived from that research.

Other than fresh are, the other major needs each body requires are fresh water and food. The water is vital for cleansing. Food actually builds physical bodies. The food is broken down into its smallest components and then used to burn for energy and rebuild new cells. We are really what we eat. The quality of food going into the body is as important as the types of and mixture of foods.

The chronic epidemic of overeating and increasing number of people developing diseases such as diabetes and heart disease is closely linked to the increase in consumption of junk food, trans-fats, sugar and processed white flour coupled with a lack of fresh fruit and vegetables. This is our physical environment and it directly affects our health.

Everyone needs to be aware that choices matter. These choices—of foods you eat and where you live can promote health or be detrimental. Lifestyle choices that can make us ill, can also work in reverse. The same factors need to be considered when trying to heal. It is no accident that many doctors tell patients to give up cigarettes due to the additives and chemical treatment of the tobacco, recommend a good diet, and focus on the need for exercise to help recover good health. If our diet is lacking any vitamins, minerals, or trace elements, this can cause illness. Any diet that is deficient in vital elements can be easily supplemented to prevent degeneration and promote health.

Unfortunately, in present society we often want instant gratification. Instead of roasting beans and brewing coffee, we walk into a shop and buy the instant variety. It is convenient to always have on hand. We expect solutions to health problems or healing to work as quickly. We expect to swallow a tablet and get well almost instantly. Aspirin and other powders may let the pain and symptoms dissolve but until the cause of any dis-ease is healed, this is no real solution. With a little understanding that problems develop over time, we as individuals can take responsibility for ourselves and our states of health through our power of choice. The daily choices amount to a cumulative outcome. It matters what, where and how we eat, whether we exercise, and how we live our lives.

I believe we choose to live under certain conditions although sometimes it feels like circumstances demand that we live in a certain way. Our level of movement and if we chose to exercise is also a matter of choice. Granted, the body can withstand quite a lot of years of neglect and even slight abuse, but eventually the ability to cope wears down. The stress of modern living, is a precursor of disease. It plagues more individuals within our society more every year. Stress is the biggest cause of diseases such as depression, heart disease, excess weight and premature aging. Stress even comes from factors like constant noise. I live on a main road in the suburbs and find that from early morning into very late at night there is noise. Noise is a vibration, which affects us on a subtle level. Constant noise is stressful to the sensitive body. Humans are adaptable creatures and we learn to selectively disregard unnecessary sounds. Children tune out to parents who constantly remind them to clean up their bedroom. Constant noise, even in the background has a negative effect on people because it is cumulative. It adds another tier to any other stress we may be suffering.

The accumulations of small problems can amount to a large pile in the end. Think of a rubbish bin. We may only have a small pile daily but the constant supply will build into a mountain over time.

The mental environment is no different and many of us believe we live in violent and difficult times. We think we have stressful times but problems are part of human life. Imagine the fear people suffered throughout history, during the wars, during the influenza epidemics or the plagues when large populations of villages, townships and entire families were wiped out?

Perhaps our idea of society is portrayed in the media in a more negative light than it really is. Imagine for a moment a young couple mugged after attending a club one night. "Proof of our violent times", you might say. When all facts are actually considered, how many people would have gone out on that particular night? How many would have returned home safely? Good news does not sell newspapers! Can you imagine the headlines reading Three thousand people in Brisbane went out to have fun last night and returned home safely? Boring!!! Nothing sensational has occurred. But a young couple who walk into a dark alley, and are mugged can be transformed into a headline and focusing on the negative outcome breeds fear. Each city has a crime rate that we could improve on but as individuals we also need to keep life in perspective. Granted that it would be quite upsetting if you personally were mugged but life does carry some risk. Part of being an adult is learning how to manage risk, decrease fear and live with low levels of stress. When we drive or ride in a car, we run the risk of being in a car accident. That is a fact. Many of us are only aware of the dangers of driving when we plan long trips, yet the risk is the same on a five minute journey as on a three week driving tour of the whole country. Once we are on the road and in a car, we are at risk but this does not necessarily mean we will have an accident. In fact over the course of most of our lives we all know some people who have never had an accident, of others who have had minor ones and of still others who have died in a road accident. Despite the road dangers, we all continue to drive cars for enjoyment as much as for necessity and convenience.

We go about our business, putting the dangers in the back of our mind, because focusing on the risk at every instance would totally paralyse us. We drive regularly without incident that we feel chances are in our favour. Accidents happen sometimes. Mishaps are a part of life. Sometimes we get an uneventful period when nothing goes wrong and other times we get a series of disappointments. Generally, life is quite good in our western world. There is no starvation, reasonable housing and generally safe living conditions . . . . yet nothing is so good that it cannot be improved. Actually, it is more a case of how we feel about what happens to us than what actually does happens. Our emotions play an enormous part in what we perceive is important in our lives.

With regard to health, there are a number of attitudes and emotions that are beneficial to the healing process, while others promote the growth of dis-ease. When we feel joy and happiness, when we feel peace and love, we are in harmony with higher vibrations, these emotions will promote health and healing. Anger, resentment, guilt, self-pity, and jealousy are all negative emotions and these work opposite. Anyone harbouring thoughts tainted with negative emotions will have negative vibrations flowing throughout their consciousness, body, mind and spirit.

Emotions are always in tune with thoughts and vibrations. You cannot be angry and at peace at the same time. You cannot be resentful, bitter, or angry, and promote the healing of your body simultaneously. This is because negative emotions are on opposing sides of the energy balance to the healing process. If you are trying to heal yourself or anyone else, it is important to be aware of and in control of emotions.

Being conscious not to harbor negative emotions in everyday life, while we are trying to heal ourselves, is particularly important because it can stop the healing process and can be particularly harmful. Feeling guilty has never cured anything but making amends and apologizing has. Sometimes we need to forgive others and ourselves as part of the healing process. Depending on the severity of to the initial issue or situation, this sounds much easier than it actually is. The amount of negative emotion attached over time can have inflated and aggravated the problem. Healing comes with letting go of those negative thoughts, ideas, beliefs, and emotions. Once this has happened, the positive energy emanating from peace of mind and heart can flow into fill the now empty space. What is good for one sphere in our life is good for our whole life. Learning to heal ourselves as individuals may one day heal the whole of society. If we all do our own part by working on ourselves, the magic will spread. Who is to say how far we will go. Planet Earth can certainly use some healing too.

PART TWO

Recipes to Heal Yourself

My recipe for health is a mixture of self-healing techniques and helps to keep me not only generally healthy but I recover quickly when I do develop a problem.

When I do get ill, and it is rarely these days since I practise these prevention techniques, I have my own set rules.

I take responsibility for myself. I also leave no stone unturned. I know health is an important part of enjoying a great life on earth and to regain it I use everything I have learnt AND everything at my disposal. I am fortunate to have attracted some wonderful health professionals into my circle of closer acquaintances or friends. One is a doctor who uses her psychic abilities to quickly find the source of the problem. There is an acupuncturist, a homeopath and a number of practitioners of essential oil massage and Reiki. I take their advice on-board and then work out my battle-plan for recovery.

FIRST I list what I am doing to recover that my mind is clear of the fact that I will recover quickly and that I am in control. All else will follow once that direction is set. To ensure I have balance in my healing plan, I work with my personal Healing Wheel.

The Healing Wheel aligns the healing process with the four cardinal directions of the Earth, the four elements, and links to the four aspects of humans.

Human development starts with the awareness of the physical. Babies play for hours with their feet. Then develop mentally—for example compare a parent's hand to their own. Emotions develop, the child begins to share, linking into the feelings of others. Eventually most humans also return to develop their spiritual nature.

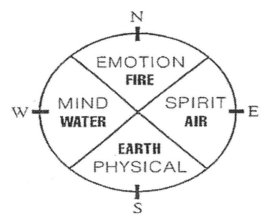

These four aspects of physical, mental, emotional and spiritual are aspects of a whole human. For perfect health, these four aspects must be in balance.

To regain vibrant health, consider using these four aspects. This means as my healing plan:

- Physical—This means take the tablets, vitamins, or do the physical procedures recommended for the particular problem that you are trying to clear.
- Mental—Consider the mental and keep as much as possible, a positive mental attitude and optimistic view of your recovery. Avoid focusing and continually talking about the pain and negatives as if they were a permanent part of you.
- Emotions—Consider your feelings. Try to overcome any fear and distract your consciousness into things that make you feel good. Read love stories, watch comedies and have friends visit.
- Spiritual—Look to your God, Source, All That Is, Allah . . . Be in touch with yourself.

All these go beyond the physical and reflect on the non-physical aspect of you. Healing manifests as a result of a combination of both the physical and non-physical. The mental aspect of healing consists of keeping a positive attitude and the belief that "this will work". The emotional aspect appreciates concern from others and connects to the feeling of being well. The spiritual aspect includes faith in the cure, faith in the healing process and its source, and finally faith in yourself as the healer.

The Healing Wheel not only ensures wholeness and balance in the healing process but also encourages the healing energies to flow with ever increasing power. Look at the diagram and imagine for a moment that the sectors or directions of the circle were power bases.

Let the healing process be like a train driving around the outside of the circle. A health problem has arisen and the train is fuelled with the power from each sector as it runs around the circle. Imagine passing the physical and taking medicine. This helps the train of the healing process go faster. If the mental sector focuses on inability to participate in social outings, this negative thinking will not speed up the healing because the energy is not positive. Other factor may slow the healing train such as negative emotions such as depression, or feeling of loneliness. Each sector affects the healing process in either promoting healing and fuelling the speed of recovery or feeding the problem and slowing recovery. Physical healing can be dynamically boosted by positive affirmations, by focusing on recovery and the giving and receiving of love. Using many avenues of healing keeps the energies continually boosting and speeds up the recovery. This is why each case of healing should be worked individually. In the case of an inevitable passing, holistic healing could mean physical relaxation techniques as well as pain medication, mental acceptance by looking forward to meeting family and friends who passed before, and feelings of peace and love.

MY PERSONAL HEALING RECIPE

STEP 1 Check it out!

If in doubt, I check my symptoms with health professionals. They have devoted their lives to medicine and healing and it would be stupid not to use that vast knowledge. I realise that our imagination will often run riot and we have a problem, look the symptoms up in a medical book we fear our head-ache is a brain tumour or the sharp pain in the breast is cancer. These negative possibilities need to be professionally tested and eliminated.

While many symptoms might relate to minor problems and are easily cleared, not checking because of fear can be harmful. This may even create a path to draw it in. I will always remember my friend Lyn who checked out every spot in case of cancer because her friend who found a lump and died of cancer. She told no-one. The sad thing is that she found the lump nine years before she died and lived in fear of dying of cancer every day for those nine years. Perhaps she would have died at that time anyway, but if she had faced the fear, the problem may have been easily fixed and she would have enjoyed those nine years or more. Sometimes it is important to consider quality of life rather than possible remaining time. For this reason, I ALWAYS recommend checking any condition with professionals to ensure possible nasties are not overlooked. Once a diagnosis is established, I can start to take control in the road towards recovery of optimum health. A correct diagnosis is important but more so is being able to picture yourself healthy. The focus must be on health!

If I am given tablets, drops or procedures I always list these first on my health plan. Belief and faith in our medical procedure will strengthen any recovery. My dad had a massive heart attack and required by-pass surgery. He recovered particularly fast after his operation as he spent many hours meditating. The difference between him and every other patient going into surgery at the time was the mental attitude he carried into the operation with him. He knew without any shadow of doubt that the operation was a big step in the process to regain his life. After he came home from hospital, the wound on his leg, where they had harvested an artery for his heart, became inflamed. His general practitioner was very thorough and immediately took tests, which confirmed that it was an infection similar to the infamous Golden Staph. Only one particular known anti-biotic could fight this particular strain. There were problems getting enough flown in from Melbourne so in the meantime another less potent drug was supplied. As the doctor did not believe in the powers of the mind, he was never told how much mental work also went into the healing. While friends and family prayed for Divine Help in the situation, Dad took matters into his own hands. He convinced his body every time he took his substitute medicine that this pill will go to the infected part and the body would be empowered to fight and kill the infection. He then visualized himself fully recovered. Already by the second day his doctor looked very puzzled. By the third day, the doctor explained that he had never seen such a fast rate of recovery with any infection given the size and severity. He could not explain the drug killing the infection and curing a condition which it should only be powerful enough to slow down. Dad just smiled and said, "maybe no-one has ever told the infection that this medicine wasn't supposed to kill it." The doctor laughed, agreed, and continued wondering at the miracle. Our medicines can be dramatically helped or hindered by our mental attitude. Your mind can be your most powerful ally in any healing process if you use it effectively.

STEP 2. My Mental Power Boosters Plan will include some or all of the following

Affirm definite recovery

Consider the professional's recommendations in the right light;

Make up a general affirmation or

Create a very specific affirmation targeting the cause;

Writing out a creative visualisation;

Choosing particular meditations or music;

Checking the habits I may need to change;

Treatments that would be beneficial or supplements

Essential oils and their application

Here are some practical techniques and exercises you can choose to work on yourself. Read them through and choose which ones to include into your plan for health and healing.

Have fun building your energy, enhancing your life, and basically promoting your vibrant health and longevity.

Using the Energy Balance

We have already learnt about positive and negative energies and how they can either promote health and recovery or cause ill health and disease. To highlight the difference, I find it both interesting and beneficial to complete this little exercise below. Simply take a page of paper (I like butcher's paper or a white board) and list these differences to focus your mind and brainstorm ideas for fun activities that will promote your health while highlighting detrimental things you may choose to eliminate.

Recipe: Hi-Lo

Split the page in two, lengthwise and name one column Low Energy and the other High Energy.

- Under the Low Energy write *dis-ease* and under the High Energy *ease* or use the words *illness* (Low energy) and *abundant health* (High energy).
- List fun and laughter, song and dance, friends and loved ones and any other pastime or enjoyable activity that can be beneficial to your healing under the high energy column.
- List sadness, jealousy, resentment, anger and the things you hate in the low energy column

It will take some time and experience to get your list balanced. Heavy metal music belongs in the Low section while lively, popular and classic music is High. Sun-showers are in the High except for hours of sunbaking which would be Low. Some medical conditions require avoidance of the sun. You will know within yourself what is right if you. Use common sense as a guide. This book assumes each of us not only has common sense but uses it and has an open, sound mind.

Recipe: Total Absorption in Fun and Laughter

Laughter and joy are a necessary part of life unless you have just been operated on and the stitches are not yet healed. In that case, I recommend hearty smiles.

- Plan to have at least one session of a minimum of 5 to 10 minutes of fun every day. The more joy, fun and laughter, the better.
- DELIBERATELY LAUGH EVERY SINGLE DAY for at least a few minutes and feel your energy rise and your spirit lift.

Granted we find it harder to find something to laugh about if we have just discovered we have a terminal illness. Especially then we should enjoy those last moments and fill them with love and laughter. The saying goes "you are a long time dead so enjoy now."

Rent or download comedies or read the Readers Digest extract Laughter is the Best Medicine. Magazines, newsagents, libraries, and book-shops are great sources of comedy.

This exercise is a great healing technique but also brilliant as a prevention exercise. People, who regularly enjoy every day, find that they can look back on a happy life. In fact, it will also give benefits to those patients who are dying.

One lady I know was diagnosed with terminal inoperable cancers throughout her whole body. She had been battling for years.

I met Jan after she had overcome many episodes and obstacles but had reached her final bout. Her solution at that stage became total acceptance that she was finally dying. She travelled throughout Europe and England for the first four of the predicted six months of her remaining life and thoroughly enjoyed her trip. On her return to Brisbane she systematically visited and contacted all her friends and family to say good-bye and rented a new VCR and television set. The remaining months of her life she spent laughing at comedies, crying with the romances and being moved with heroics as she filled the long night hours with videos. She forgot her illness and pain as much as she could and focused on enjoying the time she had left. Although laughter did not cure Jan, it gave her temporary escapes from her situation and she passed away peacefully. In his book, Mind Power, author John Kehoe documents a case of laughter actually curing a man who had been suffering from a terminal illness.

Recipe: Thoughts and Feelings

- Throughout the day consciously stop and think about what you are thinking about and how you are feeling. If you are feeling down, change your thoughts to lift your spirits.

Our thoughts are linked to our feelings. When we are smiling and happy we are thinking happy thoughts and when we learn of sad news our energies and face drop. We cannot think miserable thoughts and be truly happy. Let us consider revenge? Being happy at the demise of an enemy? Is that truly happy?

After practicing this for a few days you will find you have learnt the secret behind self-motivation is controlling your own mind to think the type of thoughts you choose. You will also come to know the greatest secret to happiness is simply choosing to think happy thoughts.

Focusing

When we concentrate or focus on something our thoughts and ideas are magnified. Just as a magnifying glass will increase the power of sunlight to focus enough light on one small spot and light a fire, so we can magnify our thoughts to concentrate on what we want. Focusing on health is particularly hard when we are ill. In fact generally we focus on our problem and our loved ones help us. The first question is "how are you?" and the next is "what does the doctor think?" When we focus on our illness, we are putting energy into it. We should focus on good health and recovery: on living life and improving not suffering and possibly death.

There is an old universal law—the Law of Attraction that states "whatever we concentrate on expands". It means that our focus grows the power of our thoughts like the magnifying glass increases the power of sunlight. Sunlight can be magnified powerful enough to start a fire. This concept makes sense. When we put extra effort into any work, we achieve more. When a student puts more time into study, then a better understanding leads to better results in tests. Whatever we focus on expands. In healing, we need to focus on getting well. If we are healthy then we should still take the time to focus on good health to maintain it.

MOST COMMON MISTAKE—Unfortunately we often focus on the negative, acknowledging "I feel tired and terrible" and giving lots of attention to the bad knee. This doesn't draw in healing but uses the mind very powerfully to attract and manifest more of the problem.

HINT: When you focus always, ALWAYS, always, ALWAYS focus on what you want and the healed condition rather than spend time feeding the detrimental problem with more fuel.

Recipe: Discovery

This exercise is quite interesting because it is important to be aware of the kinds of things we spend our time thinking about.

1. Make a small diary in either a notepad or on a few sheets of paper. As long as it portable enough for notes.
2. As often as you can throughout the day, write down a note on what you are thinking about and what your main focus is. It is not necessary to scribe every thought. A couple of times through the morning and again through the afternoon will be sufficient. Note the main ideas not every single word of every thought. You will have a list at the end of the day reflecting the major ideas and concerns that you thought about.
3. Take some time and analyse your thought patterns.

The list is for private use only and can be discarded once the information is analysed.

Are the thoughts focused on your work, other people, or what was on television last night? If you are ill, were you focusing on recovery or are you preparing for the time when you will get worse? Although we have to be realistic in any situation, it does not help to dwell on the negative. One can also go too far into the positive by constantly chanting I am well, I am well, . . . until we lose our mind. Find the happy medium. This exercise can be repeated for a few days for more patterns to be more easily recognized. Spend a day or two discovering your self-talk and you will get to know yourself. Most people are surprised at the focus of their thoughts. Using that as a basis, apply the knowledge in a sensible way. Choose to think constructive thoughts, increase the energy in your life and work towards abundant health.

Recipe: Focus on Healing

Spend 5 minutes each day alone with your thoughts on the positive healing that is taking place. Best times are when you first wake up and just before you go to sleep at night.

This exercise should be part of every person's health practice.

Focusing the mind is quite a simple task once we have taught it that we are the boss. We choose what we should think about. We focus on our healing and stop our mind from wandering from that point. In the first few sessions, you will find that you may begin to think of your healing and abundant health by watching in your mind's eye as your condition disappears. And then you will find you are thinking about something someone said, or what was in the movie last night, and you will have lost track.

If this is hard to do for the first few times, be gentle with yourself. Getting upset or angry at your initial lack of concentration will not help. Just guide your mind back to the point of your focus. After a week or two of doing these five-minute sessions once when you awaken and once just before you sleep at night, you will find them easy. You will then also begin to realise that you have developed the mind power of concentration.

As the mind thinks in pictures, it is important to have clear images that involve some sort of action. If you are on medication for an infection picture yourself taking the medicine and the infection shrinking in size and your body returning to normal. Hold the image of normal and feel your recovery. Feel, LIVE the relief or the thankfulness for the healing. The more energy you put into the exercise the more powerful the healing will be.

Focusing can be used to heal others. If you are trying to heal a loved one by focusing healing thoughts, be aware that we cannot force our choices on someone else. You can send healing. Accepting is up to them. When you are aware that you can be focusing healing energies but your target is free to choose to accept that help or not, takes the pressure out. Just as we cannot be hypnotised into doing something we would not normally do, so we cannot force others to act contrary to their own subconscious desires. I know when I am not doing it right because I get a headache.

Recipe: White Light

As illness is seen in the mind/spirit or psychic as an absence of light, many healers focus on sending white light.

- Breathe out three times, relaxing more each time.
- Imagine the diseased area or other person or you, flooded from above in white light.

Do this for a single session of 10 to 20 minutes or daily five minutes for a period of a week. Although I am told we cannot overdose on this, I find I am guided in its use and I just stop when it is enough.

Love

Love is one of the strongest human emotions. For love, we will trade our lives and our souls. It has so many aspects and is both so complicated and so simple that whole books can be written about the subject. It has been said that love is the answer to every question.

Wars are fought about love. Soldiers fight for love of country, for love of people they think they are protecting. People fight for ideas and values. Entrepreneurs trade their lives for love of money, power, and position; politicians for love of the people's attention and prestige. Scientists work tirelessly for love of knowledge in the pursuit of their chosen field. There is love everywhere. Giving, channelling and sending love can produce miracles in healing because when illnesses show up in our lives it is often through the lack of love.

If we do not have enough love for ourselves, we may unconsciously neglect or abuse our bodies and this can lead to a vast variety of illnesses. If we think we are not loved, we get ill so that friends and family prove us wrong by showing they care. Love and health are intertwined. I have been involved with healing ceremonies that left me feeling totally and unconditionally loved and at peace. I have found that love and healing are synonymous. Love can heal more than just a broken heart. Some of the healing which I have done for terminal patients has been filling the need for love within the soul.

Love then takes away the fear of dying and the inevitable passing on is peaceful.

We do not need to be on death's door to get this love. It is all around. The religions tell us that Divine love is unconditional and omnipresent. We tune in to this love when we are healing. Whether we are looking for peace to move on after a broken heart, understanding to continue in a difficult situation or just want to mend our sore elbow, the energy of love is available and can help.

Although love alone will heal a broken bone, it is important to get the limb set straight by a doctor as this will guide the bones as they knit back together and heal. We certainly are not showing ourselves love if we make ourselves suffer needlessly and do not take advantage of marvellous healing techniques in conventional medicine.

Unconditional love knows no lack or limitation and neither does perfect health. Both are the natural, available and intended to be drawn on by one and all. To let the love flow back into our bodies, mind and life, we need to only realise it is there and open up.

Recipe: Replacing Lack with Love

- Sit quietly in a place where you will be alone and not disturbed for about 10 to 20 minutes.
- Imagine your skin as a shell.
- Above your head is the sun and it is shining beautiful golden light down into your body. As the energy flows down, this golden light transforms into a pink liquid, which fills your body from the toes up. The pink liquid and the golden light are Infinite Love from the source of all Goodness and Love within the universe. The pink liquid feels warm, soft, and soothing as it fills every part of your body: even out to the tips of your fingernails and the end of every hair on your head. With the pink liquid comes peace and tranquillity.
- Slowly return your consciousness to the present while retaining the peace, tranquillity, and love.

Love is the energy that makes the laying on of hands and psychic healing work. The healer becomes a channel for love much like a dynamo becomes a transformer or energy booster. The healer is not the source but has the ability to bring an increased amount through. Generally, the energy comes out of the palms of the hands, that is why we lay our hands on the subject being healed. The hands do not actually have to touch the subject. In one of my most spectacular healing sessions, my hands were about two inches or five centimetres away from the target. The energy passing through me throughout the session was so powerful that I felt as though I had had a mild electric shock and this remained for some time afterwards. There was no pain and a true miracle occurred. The condition threatening to cause blindness *mysteriously* disappeared.

Recipe: Sending Love

- Think of someone or something you particularly love.
- Feel the energy flowing.
- You can transfer to another target. By this I mean, transfer the feeling of love to another person who you may not initially have loved but who requires healing.
- Quietly say the words "I love you" or just the word "LOVE". Words have great power especially when emotionalised.
- Imagine whatever means love to you being sent on, while knowing whatever you send out will return to you many fold.

All the philosophers and religions tell us this. Healing with love in this way should not deplete the healer but empower him/her.

We all find it easy to send love to someone we like or love. We find it more challenging to love our body when it is sick by sending the illness love. How can I love my tumour, you may ask yourself? How can I love my joints when they have paralysed me in pain with arthritis? How can I love my enemy who has hurt me? Why? The answer goes back to the energy balance. Illness and disease are part of the low energy side; part of the lack while love is the side of healing and abundance.

When we send love to our disease whether it is depression, sore toe, or any other disorder including hurt feelings, we are restoring the balance of energy and promoting health. To put it in very simple terms: if the illness is bad and hate is bad then the two *'bads'* add up to *'one worse'*. Love on the other hand is ultimate good so 'one bad' and 'one good' makes a 'nothing' and wipes out the illness.

Healing often occurs in an instant but it may take practice and patience waiting until it manifests into the physical.

Freddy may be cured from his diabetes but will continue to have a high sugar reading until the healing manifests in his body. Until his doctors also find out that he is cured, he has to keep looking after his insulin levels. The time difference is simple. The physical naturally lags behind the mental. We have to think of a new car before we buy one. We walk down the street, smell coffee and decide we want a cup. The idea comes first and the actual real episode follows. This is why diets that tell us what we are not allowed to eat often fail. We think of all the things that we are not allowed to eat, make ourselves hungry craving for that which our mind is focusing on. Our thoughts become real. As a result, we break the diet and resume eating or we feel deprived.

Affirmations

Affirmations work for and against us, always consistent with our thoughts. Most of us know what affirmations are and we have all used them in our lives but often do not realise it. How many people affirm that they never remember names? Introductions often run like this:

"John Smith, this is Mary Jones".

"Hi, glad to meet you. You know I'm terrible with names".

Meanwhile the mind says:

'I will apologies now that I will never remember your name'.

We actually affirm to the mind that we are hopeless in this remembering game just to make sure we will forget!

Affirmations are statements we use repeatedly to program our mind. One single thought passes through the mind like the constant flow of thoughts we have every day, all day long. When we build a belief into our minds or let others build one for us, we repeat the message until it flows down into the subconscious storage. Our mind is much like an iceberg.

One tenth is floating in clear view and that one tenth is the conscious mind we think with. Beliefs are held in the subconscious below the water line. To get into the subconscious the same thought has to be repeatedly spoken, either verbally or silently in the mind. Then it builds power and spirals down through the mind into the subconscious permanent memory. Once any fact is in our permanent memory we know it, we then have our belief. Think back to how you learnt your multiplication table at school? Repetition! One plus one is two and even people with amnesia who have forgotten their name will know that one plus one is two!

Did you know that, repetition programs the mind? Take note of advertisements on TV. There will be one advertisement and shortly afterwards a cut-down version of the same advertisement to keep the image alive with repetition. Airtime is expensive and the advertisers know why they repeat the adverts, it affirms the message in the mind of the potential customers. Advertising is measured and justified as effective in increased dollar sales. If it did not work, the market price would not be so high. Affirmations can be used just as effectively for healing.

The mind thinks in pictures. We often picture our mind as a machine behind our brain. This is because our mind cannot think in concepts, ideas, or words. It thinks in pictures. We may see a formula on a blackboard but that is the formula written as a picture. Ideas come in the form of energy and either manifest as pictures in our mind or as written words that we can read.

> **One very important fact:**
>
> **The mind works in pictures**
>
> **AND**
>
> **there is no such thing as negative pictures.**

Think of your bed and you will instantly have the image or a picture of your bed in your mind. If you are told not to think of a spacecraft, an apple, and London Bridge then those images still pass through your mind. But I wrote not to think of certain things, yet your mind still quite naturally pictured them. The mind thinks in pictures and cannot draw negative pictures. A negative picture is a blank nothing and tells us just that—nothing. We have to take the positive cigarette and draw a red line through it to make the NO SMOKING sign. We need to literally show what we mean.

Because the mind works in pictures, affirmations MUST be in the positive or they will work opposite to what is intended. This may sound confusing so here is an example. Imagine the case of George. He has to bring a cup of coffee to his boss who has one of the international heads of the company with him.

George tells himself 'I must not spill the coffee' and fills his mind with pictures of coffee all over the boss, the desk, and himself. Despite his fears, George wants to make a good impression for future career advancement. He has actually set himself up for failure within his own mind and established an energy flow to follow that path. He will generally be successful in achieving his visualised outcome depending on his level of emotion. It will take lots of effort to come into the office and not spill the coffee or only limit the accident to a little in the saucer. He will be tense and possibly too nervous to think of little else beside the task ahead for him. The impression he will create is the exact opposite of what he wanted but totally consistent with the picture he had built into his mind: that he is hardly capable to get the coffee and definitely not able to climb the corporate ladder.

What he should have done is to control his nervousness by breathing out three times. With each breath, he should have imagined his nervous feelings flowing out the bottom of his toes and calmness flooding in. Imagining the cup landing perfectly in front of the boss would have helped. So would silently affirmbing the words 'calm and efficient, calm and efficient, calm and efficient'. Can you imagine the difference?

Instead of having to fight himself and the problem he would have helped control the situation and turned it to his advantage. George would have created the exact image of efficiency, which he pictured.

Affirmations can let us be our own best friends or our own worst enemy. For health matters, that difference can have life and death consequence. Ann was diagnosed with cancer in the colon. She had her operation and desperately said she wanted to live as she had just become engaged to the type of man that she thought she always wanted but never thought she could marry. The affirmation that she repeated constantly was *"I will not die"*. I explained the principal of mind pictures and the vital point why she should change her words into the positive—*"I will live. I am fully recovered. I am happily married and cancer free"*. Our words manifest in the physical and the body reflects the mind's pictures.

There are only 3 simple rules for making effective affirmations.

1. They must be positive statements.
2. They must be in the present tense.
3. They must be repeated to be effective.

Affirmations must be in the present because tomorrow never comes. *"I have vibrant health"* is a powerful statement and means I have vibrant health NOW. *"I will get better"* lacks commitment. It puts the idea somewhere into the future and even sounds lame in comparison.

Dr Emile Coué is famous for his work with one affirmation that he taught all his patients. He proved its effectiveness because this is the only additional treatment he used with his conventional medicine. His recovery rates were many times better than that of his colleges.

Recipe: Everyday Affirmation

- Every morning on waking, every lunch-time, and every evening last thing before going to bed do this affirmation.
- Say 25 times the magic words. "Every day in every way I'm getting better and better".

World-renowned metaphysical healer, Louise Hay has published a wonderful book called *Heal Yourself*. This little magic book lists health problems, their probable mental causes, and the specific affirmations for healing. The underlying theme of her work is love and formation of the new thought patterns. Although I personally do not believe only our thinking everywhere always causes all health problems, I always consider her affirmations in healing schedules. Many times, I will incorporate her affirmation-cure. At other times, I am intuitively told that for some particular case, this may not be the answer. It comes to me as a feeling of coldness if the affirmation is inappropriate for the client and intense heat if the affirmation is fitting. Our mind is mysterious and often we do not know it as well as we suppose we do. When health becomes a problem, I would rather double-kill. I sometimes recommend the use of a specific affirmation which has been known to clear the problem in others even though it may not feel as though is the complete answer. For those specific affirmations I go to the expert—Louise Hay.

Recipe: Specific Affirmation

- Take your particular problem and focus on the positive answer. Learn about the cure.
- Write a specific affirmation for your unique situations and repeat it three times per day 25 times or in a block of 5 minutes.
- Remember to keep in the positive, present and when it looks, sounds and feels right, repeat it often.

Here are a few examples of helpful affirmations:—

I have a great memory and recall things easily.
I am calm and balanced.
Love. I am love.
Abundant health is my birth right.
Life is never-ending joy.
Pain is the healing process at work.
Good food energises my body to radiant health.
I am healthy, wealthy and loved.

Your Personal Environment

Every person's environment can be divided into different aspects of the physical, mental and social. Physical is the place we live in. It matters not whether it is a one-room apartment or a country mansion so long as we are happy and in a state of ease. Being within our financial means has an important effect on the stress levels in our lives. If we are beating the Jones's by living in a huge house while we can only afford the front doorknob, maybe we need to rethink.

Another aspect of the physical environment is the Principal of Order. Anyone suffering from depression, low self-esteem or any lasting illness will probably have areas in the house or apartment that are in a mess. It may be the cupboards that no-one sees or the draws of the desk. No one else may see our mess but WE KNOW where it lurks and need to clear it out.

One important point is that mess is like values. It is a subjective belief and that means a personal judgement. There are levels of mess and we have personal gauges. Look at any child's room. The child will know it is clean and tidy but mother will see mess. In our body as in our mind, order is synonymous with health. A healthy body is clean and in order. When something is wrong we get the body fighting back. Toxaemia, obesity and allergies are conditions of a body out of order. They are also conditions requiring cleansing.

Recipe: New Broom

Find a place in your physical environment and clean up while thinking of the order you are creating.

The physical has an effect on our mind/spirit self. Know in your heart that the universe is run with divine order. The planets all follow their orbit within the solar system. A new broom sweeps cleaner than an old one because of the novelty and so we make a new start by sweeping out some sort of mess and bringing order back into our lives. We link ourselves to the divine order of the universe by using the same principals. We shower and wash our bodies: rains wash the dust off trees and buildings. We link the small universe of our little bodies to the same energies within the greater universe. Abundant health is part of the natural order of all things. Look at the great, untouched rainforests. The beauty and complete balance: all naturally healthy.

Our mental environment is our general attitude. Attitude depends on the goals we have set for ourselves.

Goal setting is so often either not done or done in a haphazard way. We all spend days and weeks planning a function but virtually no time planning our lives. Do we ever really plan our recovery when we get ill?

The major healing method I teach in this book is applying a plan to health. Setting a goal for great health should be a vital part of everyday life but we only remember our health when we have lost it. NOW I will give you THE GOOD NEWS. If we know how to heal ourselves, how to set goals and achieve them, we can not only regain our lost health BUT insure that we keep it. This works within the natural limits of nature. The human soul may be immortal but our body has some physical limits. Setting a goal to live for 200 years may be a little ambitious today but as our medicine improves and we actively practice disease prevention techniques, our life spans are constantly increasing, so who knows? A few years into the future our children or grandchildren may consider a life span of 150 to 200 years as normal.

Recipe: Discover Your Goals

To manifest goals they must first be discovered and/or invented.

Goals can be categorized into lifelong purpose, long-term, short-term and immediate. This sets a timeframe for their achievement. Without a set time frame, they are only wishes and dreams. They may materialise but your mind will not consider the thought as a serious order.

- To discover your lifelong goals, imagine writing your epitaph. What would you like to have achieved in your lifetime. This is not an exercise in morbidity or a wish to die but allows the purpose of life to come forward.
- To discover your long-term goals, decide what you want to happen within the next ten years.
- To reveal your short-term goals set the time frame for six months to one year.
- To decide your immediate goals, just list them as they flow out of your current needs and wants.

Once the goals are established, the work of energising them into existence begins. It should be noted that the process of designing the complete range of goals can take several days and will change as time passes. New goals will emerge and others will pale in their need or want to be fulfilled.

Life goals and long term goals should be written on paper and placed in a safe place for them to manifest in their own time.

Shorter-term goals can be manifested using the Gold Card. Work on no more than three to five goals at any particular time.

Recipe: Gold Card

I have found that goal-cards are worth many times their weight in gold. When correctly applied they can eventually give us anything our heart desires (if we feel it is in our best interest). For this reason, I call them GOLD CARDS.

- Use one card for each goal or put several on the one card
- Write clearly
- List what you want and why
- Read the card many times throughout the day to focus your mind and let the universal energies know you are serious.

Sometimes It is good to take the ideas further and consider ways of how you think you can achieve the goals then follow through. Often it is good to leave the process to the universe but then act on ideas that you get. Nothing will be achieved without action. If you want a slim and trim body then notice an advertisement that catches your eye and it is part of the solution, this is your prompt to follow through and make it happen.

The process of repeated affirmations is much like playing in the rain as a child. When we draw a line with a stick in the dirt water quickly fills it and we create a small river. The more we work with the stick retracing that original line the bigger our river becomes AND more importantly, once started, if left alone it will still continue to grow but it takes repeated effort and some action. Keep up the mental work to focus the direction of the goal.

Norman's recipe he used to program his mind and attract his goal manifested his car:

1. A small car of my own;
2. So, I do not get wet in the rain.
3. I want it before I start back at school in February,
4. I can get an extra job to pay for it.

You can adapt the recipe to anything in your life. Here is a recipe you might chose to lose weight:

1. I weigh 60kg (whatever is correct for you).
2. To be the correct weight for height, fit and trim.
3. I will look stunning at my wedding
4. I eat only fresh health producing foods, walk twice daily and drink water instead of snacking between meals.

Note this warning, if you do not make the goal you will never achieve it. We hear stories of people who were told they would never walk again who are now walking. You can be bold. Aim for the sky because you can only go as far as your aim and no one step further but if this process is new for you and your belief or faith is low it might be good to start on something small and achieve that, then slowly build up to the really big goal. I started by visualising parking spots and green lights everywhere I went. When that happened I was on such an emotional high that my belief in myself soared and I was able to manifest much bigger ideas and had the belief that I would be successful to fuel my desires. Then it became difficult to understand when something didn't happen like I planned.

Cheat Version

Dream often of what you want and feel like you already have it leaving the time-frame to the universe to provide. Just feel great about the result!

Points to remember are:

- Keep an open mind and positive attitude. Being positive that you cannot do this does not count!
- Give it time to become real. We plan a banquet and then need time to prepare, cook, and decorate. The only thing instant is the idea but we need to hold the idea. Just as the banquet needs constant bolding of the final goal to guide the work, so we need to hold our goal to guide the energies to eventual success.
- The more vibrant and positive you make your images the brighter the picture. Emotions are mental catalysts. They are like the glue that holds the idea together and gives it a strong base. Therefore, the more emotions you put in the more power you add to your goal.
- The more repetitions you make the more power you get. Hit a rock often enough with a sledgehammer and it will be pulverised.

Consider your social environment too. Your social environment consists of the people who surround you. That means our family, friends, acquaintances, and colleagues. There is a wise old saying that goes something like this—*"show me your friends and I will show you what you are"*. It has been reported that we make the same amount of money as the three people closest to us. This is because money is another form of energy and like draws like. In the area of health it is also important that we look at the energy of others surrounding us. We need vibrant individuals who will lift our spirits and help us not vampires that deplete our resources.

Recipe. My Mates Analysis

- Write down the list of names of the people with whom you spend most time;
- Write 3 to 5 words or ideas to describe each.
- Imagine them offering to spend a week with you. How do you feel about the prospect? How do they make you feel? Do they lift your energy levels or your temper?

Your list might be short

1. Lisa—bright, bubbly, a bit dumb but a good sport.
2. John—tired, stuck in the past, lazy and a bit of a drip.

And how they make you feel might be simple and clear

1. Lisa—positive person & great to be around.
2. John—An energy vampire & draining.

Sometimes it isn't so clear or it is family members who we feel obliged to hang around, so we might need to change how we feel about them. That is our only point of power. While it may be hard to change how we think and feel personally, it is impossible to change someone else, especially if they don't want to.

Recipe: Change my mates

- Write down the positives about the person you are having difficulty with
- Ask yourself what it is specifically about them or their actions that you have difficulty with
- Listen to your answer and act on them
- Put the factor into perspective—if it is small let it go—if it is big, actively work through it
- Realise that how you approach the subject of any change has an impact on the outcome
- If you need them to modify their behaviour use the "when you, I feel process" . . .

The following process is amazing for getting to the heart of a problem without confronting or blaming. It is good to use when you are having difficulty with another person and you cannot tolerate something but wish to retain the friendship.

Let us assume that your friend has the habit of picking his nose and it grosses you out. The solution would go like this.

Example Recipe: When you—I Feel

- Be clear about the behaviour or expressions you need to clear out
- Tell your friend—"When you . . . pick your nose, I feel like . . . running away from you".
- Explain your problem—"It makes my stomach flip and I feel it is totally rude and horrible behaviour."
- State your solution—"I would appreciate it if you could not do that while you are with me"
- State the consequence—"If you do I will have to walk away from you because I just cannot tolerate that behaviour.
- Remind them of what the outcome will cost them. "I love you and don't want to lose our friendship over this."
- Request them to act—"Do you think you could change your habit for me?

This process puts the responsibility for change on your friend and communicates your feelings. They have the power to act and you remain strong and powerful too. Of course the choice lies with them but because the power also lies with them they feel they have nothing to lose. They feel that they are in control and are more likely to do what you want than leaving them no choice. If you degrade their behaviour they are more likely to become defensive and fight.

Looking after Yourself & Your Body

Body and life are vitally interconnected. Your body is really, really important. You need it to function here on the planet. It is very precious and quit fragile. It isn't like a set of clothes where you can get a replacement and continue your life here. When your body dies, you move on.

People who believe in reincarnation will admit that your life, this time around, is limited to the current body. Even if you know that you have an unlimited spirit and will come back to another life—it is another life. Not this one, here and now, with this family and these friends, this job, this house and this body. You and I are inside our personal bodies now. That means this point in time and place in space. Whether we think of our body as the temple for the soul or we just drag this 'lump' around with us, this is all we have. It is precious and deserves care.

That is an excellent reason for looking after the vehicle that will carry you through this life. When your vehicle is demolished you can drive it no further and die.

> ### Recipe: Common Sense body action steps
>
> - Feed it good, nutritious food
> - Drink sufficient clean water
> - Have adequate rest and recreation to manage stress
> - Exercise regularly
>
> (Before beginning any strenuous exercise program—have a physical check-up with your doctor and discuss the program with him/her. Even young people can have heart problems and the point of exercising is to prolong life **NOT to extinguish it.**)

Vital Oxygen

There are a number of necessities to life. Good food and clean water are vital but oxygen is the most vital requirement a body has. You can go many weeks without food, days without water but only minutes without oxygen.

Not only is it vital to get air, the quality of that air is also very important. Nobel Prize winner Dr Warburg tested the effect of oxygen on living cells and his research proved that depriving and reducing oxygen would turn healthy cells malignant. This could suggest that pollution may be the cause of some of the cancers of today BUT MORE IMPORTANTLY, the research proves that oxygen is definitely vital to maintaining health.

Breathing is a natural and automatic rhythm that each of us instinctively follows. But . . . breathing deeper enhances the amount of oxygen taken into the body and is beneficial for several reasons. It clears the mind, improves the quality of blood, complexion and overall health.

Taking a walk in nature enhances the oxygen in your body, but so do breathing techniques from the discipline of yoga. Yoga belief is that life is in the breath. Here are some of the recipes you might like to try.

Recipe: Complete Breath Sitting

- Sit cross-legged on the floor (or straight on a chair if you find it difficult).
- Breathe out through the nose while contracting you abdomen;
- Slowly breathe in while pushing the abdomen out to let air into the bottom of the lungs.
- Continue breathing in and expand the chest. This will mean that the abdomen will contract a little.
- Continue to inhale slowly as you raise the shoulders to let air into the top of the lungs.
- Hold the breath for the count of three.
- Slowly breathe out through the nose again while contracting the abdomen.

Repeat the exercise three to ten times.

Setting up a regular schedule for breathing exercises will benefit body mind and spirit.

Eventually try to inhale, hold, and breathe out for the same length of time, perhaps even extend the time. Concentrate on the vital oxygen going throughout your body.

Recipe: Complete Breath Standing

- Stand with feet slightly apart, arms by your side.
- Breathe out through the nose while contracting the abdomen, relaxing and dropping all muscles.
- Slowly breathe in while pushing the abdomen out to let air into the bottom of the lungs while raising the arms slowly.
- Continue breathing in and raising the arms slowly as the chest expands. The abdomen will contract a little.
- Continue to inhale slowly as your hands meet above your head.

- Hold the breath for the count of three.
- Slowly breathe out through the nose again while your arms come back down by your sides.

Repeat five to seven times.

This exercise is done in a slow dance-like motion of continual flow.

Exercise: Cleansing Breathe

- Breathe in at the specific ratio of in for one to hold for four and then out for two.
- If you are slowly counting, then it would be as follows. Breathe in for the count of 2, hold for the count of 8, and breathe out for the count of 4. This creates a vacuum effect that rids the body of toxins. Naturally, the cycle is repeated for each breath to be complete.

Repeat 10 times.

Please note that all three exercises are separate. They do not have to be all done three times every day.

The power of healing with oxygen

One woman in America claims to have actively cleared herself from a type of lymphatic cancer by doing breathing exercises between 2 and 4 am every morning. She would flood her body with oxygen, every morning, when it was at its most vulnerable. She had studied circadian rhythms.

Circadian rhythm is the name for our body's natural inbuilt clock or biorhythm. Energy levels and electrical vibrations are at the lowest in the small hours of the morning (generally dropping to the minimum between 2 and 4 am). At this time, we have least resistance to disease and she knew that any disease, virus or bacteria will thrive most when the body's natural defences are at their lowest. While doing her breathing exercises, she concentrated her mind on flooding her whole body with the beneficial oxygen which she thought would then starve the disease of the room to grow. It is important to note that the breathing exercise was one of a number of things she did. The others included creative visualisations, meditations, a cleansing diet, and acupuncture. The important result was her return to abundant health. (The doctors called it a remission.)

Becoming and Staying Fit

When we are fit and have good muscle tone we feel healthy and we look good. Yes, we know how it feels but everybody else knows how it looks. Sometimes achieving fitness is a gradual process particularly following a long illness. Fitness does not happen overnight but with gradual exercise the muscles will improve.

There are many gyms, personal trainers and programs that can be followed or moulded to individual needs. Here is one—the "Royal Recipe" for fitness-

The Royal Canadian Air Force developed the 10BX program for women—5BX for men. It sets out charts and exercises, which begin with the easiest variety and lowest number. It then recommends that participants work gradually up the levels according to their own body's ability. A very innovative yet overweight teacher first taught me this program as a school sport. She also introduced us to yoga relaxation techniques, which have helped me tremendously over the years. (I mentioned before about checking with a medical practitioner prior to beginning any exercise or fitness program.)

Stretching for fitness

The yoga discipline recommends stretching as an excellent way to get healthy muscle tone. Stretching, like building fitness, is done one small step at a time. In fact, all exercises should be gradually worked up to. Dr Deepac Chopra recommends doing half the number of anything you are capable of doing. If you can run four miles, run two. Gradually you will build your level of fitness and find that you could actually run ten. At that stage, you should be running five. In the same way, the following stretching exercise may take some weeks to achieve. Be patient and persistent.

Recipe: Complete Stretch

- Stand with legs slightly apart.
- Reach up to the sky as far as you can while breathing in and hold both the breath and the position.
- Bend at the hips and slowly stretch down to the floor while breathing out. (The aim is to get the palms of the hands onto the floor).
- Return to normal position.

Repeat three times very slowly. Gradually over time, make the holds longer until you can hold for the count of 20.

Disguised stretches or Active games

Disguised stretches are games like drawing circles and figure eights into the air. These symbols are a sign of the never-ending cycle of life and the infinity of the universe. Physically getting really into the game will make the body more flexible and remove toxins from nooks and crannies. It will also bring the energy body into balance.

Try this recipe alone or with friends to have some laughs. After all—
laughter is also good medicine!

Recipe: Loosening Up

- Stand with legs slightly apart.
- While keeping the rest of the body still, with the toes of one foot draw one to three circles in the air. First anti-clockwise then clockwise. Repeat by drawing a figure eight first one way then the other. This frees the joints of the foot.
- Next, using the heel draw one to three circles in the air, first anti-clockwise then clockwise; then draw a figure eight first one way then in reverse. This works on the knees.
- Draw one to three circles in the air with the knee. First anti-clockwise then clockwise; then draw a figure eight first one way then the other. This may take a little balance, or the aid of a solid object to lean on, but will work on the hip joint.
- Now repeat the whole procedure with the other leg.
- Fingers are normally quite nimble but you can draw a circle and figure eight with each individually.
- Work the wrists by drawing the signs with the hands.
- Exercise the shoulders, one at a time, by drawing with the elbows.
- Drawing with the shoulders one at a time, to exercises the muscles in the neck and shoulder blades.
- Keeping shoulders and feet still, draw the circles and eights with your hips.
- Finally, loosen the tension from the neck by gently moving the head in exactly the same rhythmic series of circles and eights.
- Stand perfectly still when finished to let the energies balance.

Repeat this exercise occasionally whenever needed.

Walking for Exercise

A flexible body also needs to have the heart pumped daily. Walking is the best all around exercise. Even heart patients are advised by their doctors to walk.

For reasonably healthy people can easily starting walking at a safe basic rate. Perhaps a 3-5 minutes warm up then 3-5 minutes brisk walking and finally another 3-5 to wind down. This can be gradually increased. Although many believe we need to only exercise three times a week, walking should be done on a daily basis. If you find walking even for a few minutes stressful when you begin, see your doctor.

For low impact exercise, the air-walking machines are fantastic. This is especially recommended for people who have suffered injuries and cannot stand the normal impact of walking. In those cases careful monitoring by a professional is recommended and taking care not to try to do too much too soon.

Walking to Lose Weight

During my undergraduate degree at university, we returned from one summer break to find one member of our group missing. In the place where Brad sat was a new young man. In the break between lectures, we began to compare grades from the previous year and the new man began to join in the conversation. Brad had lost so much weight we had not recognized him. He looked fit and marvellous and not at all like he had starved himself. Brad explained his recipe. His secret was walking. He gradually over a period of a week built up to walking 10 miles every day. Each morning he would walk about 2 hours before work. At lunchtime, he spent an hour walking and the rest he did after 6pm. The weight had just dropped off him. I must also mention Brad is armed service personnel and was healthy and fit before he started. A radical and impossible cure for many but it worked for him. We are all individuals and have the freedom to choose to follow another's example or to reject their ideas because they do not suit our particular situation. Our group also included Ben who wanted to lose weight but did not consider even walking 1 kilometre daily because he was too busy with his work. He bought an exercise bike so that he could stop at any time without having a long walk back home. We must do that which is right for each of us as individuals!

Walking backwards

One of my mentors visited China and found very mature aged students at a university for retired folk. The odd thing they did every morning before class was walking backwards. They explained that it helps the brain because it is working a natural process in reverse. It also decompresses the spine relieving pressure and causes laughs. I do it in the park when I can see there is no-one in front of me. My neighbour from Sri Lanka practices it too and we smile as he jogs past the house every morning—sometimes going forwards and sometimes going backwards. Apparently he has been doing this for decades and it must be working for him. He looks like a fit 50 year old and is in his late 70s.

Walking to relieve depression

Walking in nature has been proven to help lift depression. The physical movement increases oxygen flow to the brain and muscle tone to the body. As the body moves—arms swing, shoulders loosen, head holds higher tension depletes. The back moves, muscles stretch and relax, inner organs are massaged and lungs expand. With increased oxygen to the brain fogginess can lift. Looking in nature generally has a relaxing effect on the mind to let it drift off with the birds and this in turn lifts spirits. An outdoor meditation of sorts! It's all good weather permitting.

I live in a sub-tropical zone and in mid—summer it really is too hot to walk outside except in the early morning or at night. Some groups meet in local shopping centres and walk through the hallways a couple of times and finally settle for a break at one of the coffee shops. They find the stores they want to visit at a later date, catch up on sales and see all the specials. They have fun. The shop-keepers love them. They provide free advertising because they tell all their non-walking friends of what is available and where.

Walking to relieve stress

Walking is low impact exercise and good for stress relief due to the natural chemistry boosts. Exercise increases endorphins—the natural feel-good hormones in the brain. Stepping up from walking and getting into very brisk walking, jogging or running will decrease stress hormones like cortisol as well and still give a natural lift to moods. Natural body chemistry can produce a natural high as a direct result of exercise.

Other stress relievers

Increasing physical fitness aids stress relief because fit people are able to withstand more stress than individuals who are inactive. However— Hectic lifestyles leave some people suffering from stress. They do not want to or cannot fit exercise into their busy lives. Move to relieve that stress? No! Tired bodies are reluctant to exercise. We may crave relaxation and feel we NEED a more passive release.

- A hot bath with a few drops of lavender oil may be the answer.

Aromatherapy oils have been used throughout the ages and a few drops of lavender into a hot bath will help relax the mind as the heat slowly works to relax the muscles. Low light and soft soothing music can help the therapy. Homemakers and mothers are often worn out by the end of the day. A hot, lavender or herbal bath can replace some of the energy the normal day has worn away by calming the tensions. Deliberately taking the time to relax will also work wonders for the self-image. Every person is special and deserves to be pampered at times. Sometimes we need to be our own best friend and pamper ourselves. Realising that this is a form of self-healing may make the procedure more acceptable.

- Try cool baths

Cool salt baths invigorate while heat relaxes. Adding minerals and/or sea salt will give extra tingle. Fully submerse at least three times. A dip in the ocean or clear mountain stream would be better. As this is not readily available to most of us, or as private, I have found the bath is an effective substitute.

- Or Massage

Stimulation can be used to clear out the cobwebs. Massage is available in various techniques—soft and relaxing, sports massage to get rid of knots in the muscles and even holistic treatments that enhance body mind and spirit. It can encompass the whole body or be restricted to particular parts like neck and shoulders or feet. One important factor with massage is trust. Bodywork is very personal. Therapeutic massage should not touch the sexual organs. Sexual massage may be relaxing or stimulating and can be healing but is within another category of healing not referred to here.

Drinking Water

The human body is said to be approximately 70% water. For it to function correctly, we have to have a certain amount within our system. Many conditions like arthritis and rheumatism, can be relieved slightly if water is increased to eight to ten glasses per day and coffee, tea and alcohol is reduced to a minimum. Joints move more freely if the body has a high water level. Fresh, clean water has the added benefit that it will flush toxins from the body. To do this, the water should be pure. Let me also add that drinking hot water rather than coffee when arising in the morning cleanses the body. In fact, it can also clear the body of excess weight, if it is sipped often enough throughout the day. The hot water puts a warm feeling into the stomach area. People who overeat often do so out of nervousness or anxiety. The hot water gives a feeling of comfort and ease. Once comfort replaces the feeling of anxiety, there is no craving for food. The first cup of hot water tastes strange but one soon gets used to it. After a day or two of sipping hot water, I began to prefer it to coffee, tea, and even my special herbal teas. Socially, it is becoming more acceptable. When I first began asking for hot water, I got strange looks from staff and friends. Now it is considered quite reasonable as more people follow the same practice.

Diet

The body needs food, water, and air to survive. These are broken down by the body and used as building blocks to replace the cells in a never-ending process of regeneration. A body can survive on very little and on small variety, if required to do so. Each body functions best when provided with good food. It then also has the best chance for surviving challenges that come along. The quality of the food we eat directly affects the quality of the body we will build. Therefore, a healthy, well-balanced diet is vital.

It was established that the health triangle is the best guide to healthful eating. Eating by quantity, most grains and cereals, fruit and vegetables, then meats and dairy products, and least fats and sugars is recommended by many dieticians. In recent times High Protein—Low Carb diets have emerged to get rid of bulging midlines. Gluten sensitivity, diabetes and many other health challenges have specific dietary recommendations that can help and sometimes even clear symptoms or the diseases themselves.

Depending on specific needs, the balanced diet, which recommended daily intake of meat and three vegetables, is sometimes not considered appropriate. It is a minefield out there.

We are now encouraged to eat less meat, consume a breakfast of either fruit and fresh fruit-juice or a cereal, drink less coffee and alcohol and at least 8 glasses of water.

More and more health professionals recommend taking daily dietary supplements. They suggest our food does not contain the nutrients we expect. Whenever food is processed, it looses nutrients. The food does not even have the quality and nutrients it should have when it is first produced. Soils are depleted of the full spectrum of minerals, varieties are bred to produce bulk, transportable goods rather than the fine tasting, and finally chemicals intrude at every stage of production.

Some recommend that, to have healthy food we should return to the practice of our grandparents and have our own vegie patch in the back yard. This may sound like a noble practice but it is not an available option for many people. As larger portions of the population live in high-rise apartment blocks, the ability to have a garden disappears. The only viable option is to supplement the diet with the necessary vitamins, minerals, and trace elements. This is like entering another jungle. Health products are generally very expensive but if they prolong life, return our good health, and promote a feeling of wellness, this is acceptable. The only recommendation, which I can add at this point, is to research well. Select particular brands of health products you feel are worth taking. It may be defeating the purpose to take supplements, which contain residual chemicals that have the potential to harm, in an effort to clear a particular condition. We need to let our brains, common sense, and intuition be our guide.

If in doubt see your medical professional. If you are on medication, letting your doctor know what else you may be taking is important. Perhaps your intake and the prescription medication could be working in opposition to one another or working the same giving you a potentially harmful overdose.

Your choice

Looking after the body is simple. Let your own body be the guide by tuning into how you feel after eating certain foods, drinking different beverages, and participating in particular activities. Keeping your own counsel and keeping everything in moderation, is still the best advice. Deciding what to do is sometimes difficult. Advice of others can be useful, however the best source of information is generally from within. You can do this by tapping or tuning in to your inner guidance system.

Tapping into the Source

When we tap into the source, into universal intelligence, we reach a deep special state of mind. It is a state of being where natural healing can occur almost automatically. It is bliss—peace, contentment—a place where everything and anything is possible. Source is unconditional love—pure energy.

According to scientists, we are made up of atoms. These atoms consist of a nucleus and electrons oscillating around them in the same way as the planets orbit around the sun. All mass is made up of tiny atoms, which form groups or clusters that make up the various elements. Let us assume the elements are the building blocks of the universe because everything is made up of elements and atoms. We are made up of the same stuff as trees, animals, rocks, whatever—just in different combinations. We have a minute amount of iron in our bodies and a large amount of water while an iron bar is almost pure iron with much, much less water. Being made up of the same stuff as the universe gives us a connection. And being made of atoms that are largely open space of electrons spinning around a nucleus makes us energy.

We are energy, just as the universe is energy. This universal energy can be harnessed for healing. It is ever present and not discriminatory. Neither good nor bad, it is just available. On that assumption, we can presume that every single one of us, no matter our race, colour, gender, or religion can tap into this source of power.

We tap in through meditation and relaxation. Once we have tapped in, we can reach the healing state of awareness. This heightens the body's ability to heal itself. It is that supreme state of awareness where miracles are possible.

Anyone who has ever experienced a miracle will have felt this special state at its most powerful. We feel it to a lesser degree when a healer comes to our aid. People who are trapped in car wrecks feel it when the rescue team arrives. The expectant mother feels the same vibration and relief in the labour-ward when the midwife or doctor arrives. With the professional help comes the expectancy that now all will be well. The mind says quietly, I am in safe hands and the healing state has been reached because tension and nervous energy is swept away.

When the panic goes away so does the confusion. Peace and order replaces the worry and the energy can work toward healing instead of against it. Anyone can reach and tune in to this healing state once the process has been learnt. Sometimes the process happens naturally. Maintaining it and remaining calm in difficult situations may be hard but this can also be achieved. My father survived his massive heart attacks because of his ability to relax and maintain that relaxed healing state of mind.

We can train ourselves to reach this deep level of relaxation. It may take time to go through the process of learning how but all training takes time and effort. The body can learn to be told to relax just as the body can learn how to run or swim.

There are many ways to relax. Directly instructing the body to relax, using a counting-down technique, and the mantra method are three methods which I will teach in this book. The state of relaxation is a scientifically measurable level of mind producing alpha brain waves. Whichever method is used to achieve the relaxation response is fine. Each way takes time to perfect but once learnt gives almost instant results. You may never have to remain calm while waiting for an ambulance during a heart attack but in daily life many situations occur that can benefit from calmness rather than panic.

Imagine you are late for an appointment and have lost the car keys. Panic will not help. Thinking clearly will. You can only think clearly when we are relaxed. No one ever thinks clear while panicking. We may stumble on a right answer through intuition but generally, we are lost in a sea of confusion. Our mind spins over the same ground repeatedly. We can learn to go beyond this by learning to relax on command.

Preparation for learning is simple.

- Find a place and a time where you will not be disturbed for at least 30 to 40 minutes.
- Lights should be dim or low.
- There should be an even temperature so that you do not need to turn the heat or ventilation up during the session.
- Play soft soothing music or have relative quietness.

These optimum conditions are for learning. Once you have mastered the conscious relaxation response, the countdown technique, or the mantra method, you can relax in a busy street in the middle of a hectic schedule. You can relax your muscles while driving or calm down and appear confident when the boss asks you into his/her office although you may not know if you will be terminated or promoted.

Recipe: Conscious Relaxation

- Lie flat on the floor or bed or sitting in a chair, which will support you in the event that you may over-relax and fall asleep. If you are lying on the floor put a pillow under the knees to take the strain off the lower spine.
- Close your eyes and begin by taking three long, deep breaths and breathing out through the nose.
- Concentrate on the out breath imagining as you breathe out, you are also breathing out stress, strains, and those things that have previously caused you tension.
- Wriggle and stretch your toes then relax them.
- Stretch your toes a second time and relax them.
- Relax the muscles in your foot. Focus on the muscles and tell them to relax. Feel how relaxed they are.
- Go to the calves of your legs to the knees and relax. Feel them sink into the floor or bed. Being relaxed, they may feel heavy, light, or as though they are not even there. You will feel whatever is right for you.
- Think of the thigh muscle and relax it. Maybe you need to contract it first and then relax.
- Now the whole of the legs are relaxed and at ease.
- Relax the buttocks.
- Move your consciousness to the abdomen and relax the inner organs.
- Relax the rectum, genitals, bladder, and the small intestines.
- Imagine the liver, spleen, colon and stomach relaxed.
- Relax the diaphragm and the chest area. Relax the lungs by breathing out gently and relax the heart.

You may find that you hear your heart beats faster and stronger. What is actually happening is that in slowing the body and concentrating the mind, you are finally hearing the body as it normally works.

- Relax the shoulders and let them sink into the floor/bed.
- Relax the upper arms, the forearms, hands, and fingers.

As you relax the arms, you may notice that as the tensions are disappearing they are leaving peace and order. Clearing the body of tensions is the way to relaxation.

- Relax the neck and run your mind down the backbone relaxing the little muscles on either side of the spine. The neck and the base of the spine generally hold a huge amount of stress.
- Relax the face, let the jaw drop slightly, relax the cheeks and the little muscles around the eyes.
- Relax the forehead and the brain.
- Your consciousness is now at the crown of the head.
- Imagine a soothing warm gold or blue liquid moving into your body. It is slowly flowing from the top of your head, filling every part of your body with relaxing balm until you reach the very toe-nails at the bottom of your feet.

Your whole body is now relaxed and at ease.

In time, you can teach yourself to imagine the magic liquid flowing down through the body and relax in a matter of seconds anywhere.

Recipe: Counting Down

- Sit quietly, breathe out three times and relax.
- Tell yourself when you reach 0 you will be perfectly relaxed.
- Begin counting backwards from 100 down to 0

At 0, you should feel yourself reaching a state of peace.

In this state of peace, there is a definite feeling of relaxation and beauty. The state is hard to describe but once you have reached it you will know and understand. If your brain waves were measured you would be showing to produce alpha brain waves. We naturally go through this level of mind whenever we wake slowly. Actual sleep is in the theta brain level and normal waking state is beta. Between the two is a relaxed state of awareness and that state of mind that is optimal for healing, the alpha state.

Recipe: Counting Down—deeper session

- After practicing for two to three days of counting from 100, begin from 90, then 80, 70 and so on until you can relax and achieve alpha brain waves at the count of 5-4-3-2-1-0. You can then relax in a matter of second. I say 3-2-1 and relax. In emergency, just relax. It works once you have trained yourself.

The training session will depend on prior conditioning and mind controls already established. I have watched two people begin this exercise at the same time and one reached the 5 to 0 level in a week. The other often found that he had to count 100 to 0 twice in the beginning and took over 6 weeks to finally reach the 5 to 0 level. We are all different and being able to train yourself quickly does not help if you never use the technique afterwards. Persist and the reward will come.

Reaching the alpha level by counting down is great for relaxation but has many further possibilities. Creative visualisations and healing meditations are improved if practicing at the alpha level. It should be the basis for any mental exercise because it is a most powerful state of mind. For self-healing it is an invaluable tool. Just learning to reach this level has cured a number of small ailments in quite a lot of people in relatively short time. Larger problems take longer. Chronic conditions like asthma can be dramatically improved.

Another way to reach the alpha relaxation state is through using a mantra. A mantra is one word recited repeatedly. Often it is an unreal word consisting of one or two separate sounds.

Recipe: Mantra Method

- Settle in peaceful surroundings with the intention to go within.
- Repeating the word quietly over and over for about 20 minutes up to twice daily. The mind will quite naturally go into the alpha state.

Ho, Om, Ah, I am, Peace, and Love are some of the sounds or words to use. My friend who has spent time in Tibet chants Om! Ma-ni pad-ne Hum! Or you can find your own. Formally learning transcendental meditation will teach the use of this technique and supply you with your personal sound.

Be patient for the benefits. They will come. Some may be in small and unexpected ways. Your appetite may be regulated. You may just begin to naturally reach for the right food and cravings for unhealthy options begin to disappear. Your life may just flow better and relationships may improve. You may just be more confident at work or stop impulse buying to let your money situation improve. Whatever helps you on your path can come about.

Using Universal Energy

Universal energy can be channelled by a person simply touching another. This technique is referred to Laying on of Hands. The healing power comes from beyond. Religions explain the source as the Supreme Power of their own faith. The exact name we give the source does not matter. People who do not feel comfortable with this idea of a Divine Force can still channel universal healing energy. Energy has no religion. By nature, it is there. IT JUST IS!!

Universal healing energy flows wherever it is needed once the doors are opened. Just as water always naturally flows down to fill the lowest point first, so the healing energies flow down to us without asking our beliefs. To access the energies we need only have a mind that is to open healing. At minimum, one that is not closed to the possibility that help may be accessible from beyond. To direct or channel them we simply choose. We can send the energy to others but cannot force it to go to anyone in particular if they do not wish to accept it. It remains everyone's free choice to receive or not.

I always ask permission before working on anyone. Most times people will approach me and ask for help. Then the issue does not arise. I have prayed for and sent healing to people who did not ask for help or believed in a Devine force, but always with the caveat "if he/she chooses to accept". Acceptance can be on a spiritual level so someone may not even be conscious and healing energy work can occur for them.

The most exciting aspect of tapping into universal healing is that each individual can help themselves. A friend had a heart bypass operation and had scars on her leg and chest. While she lay in recovery she started channelling healing energy through her hands over her wounds. The areas she could reach with her hands healed much faster and cleaner than the rest. IF she had known that she could have simply visualised her hands over the scars outside of her reach, she could have worked on all her wounds. As it was it proved for all of her friends and family, just how powerful an impact hands on healing made.

Recipe: Laying On of your own Hands

- Sit or lay quietly, while thinking of what it is you are doing.
- Know that healing energies are all around you because the whole universe is energy in constant flow.
- Put your hands on the physical part of yourself that needs healing—letting the healing energies flow in through the top of the head and through to the ailing area.

We sometimes put our head in our hands when we feel depressed. When we do this, we are instinctively letting the healing energies in.

The flow of energy works better if the spine is kept straight throughout the session. Time span for this exercise varies. It may last for 2 to 3 or 20 to 30 minutes. It stops when we want to stop. Let your feelings be your guide.

It is interesting that one palm on the forehead and the other in the back of the neck will generally automatically make the brain produce alpha brain waves. This is a little awkward to do for yourself while keeping the spine straight but is quite easy to do for someone else and will relax them quickly.

Healing Others

When we heal through this method, we are stimulating the energy field of the client. The name given to this energy field is our aura. It vibrates around and through us and takes on a colour depending on our thoughts, mood, and life in general. Although these colours are invisible to the naked eye, we are often aware of them on a subtle level. We know instinctively when someone looks unhealthy just as we describe and see people with a bubbly personality.

Recipe: Laying Hands on Another

Having the patient sit on a chair with their back to you is easiest.

- Simply place hands, palms down on or a few inches above the crown of the head.
- After a few minutes move your hands to rest lightly on or above the shoulders.

It is not necessary to move directly to the area that is ailing as energy flows naturally to the place of least vibration.

Healers generally know through inner guidance, if they need to put their hands elsewhere. The one being healed must be completely comfortable with this procedure and with the healer. I feel I must mention here that NO healer I have ever known has directly put their hands on any sexual areas. Sexual energies may be specifically used in the healing of marriage and relationship problems but are not for general healing as used in this context. If there is healing required in reproductive organs, holding the hands a few inches away will work even for healers who normally prefer direct touch on shoulders or others parts of the anatomy. I would be more than just suspicious of anyone laying hands directly on any part of my body that I am not fully comfortable with. For this reason and particularly with complete strangers it is sometimes advisable to have a third person present.

Laying on of hands, mental healing imaging, psychic healing or spiritual healing are all names for the same method of work. They take universal energies to stimulate the vibration level of the individual to be healed. One mysterious point to this form of healing is the results and side issues cleared up. Depression, frustrations, hopelessness, and desperation can be reversed. Stress and tension can be relieved. When this happens, other areas of life also change for the better. There is no guarantee exactly what will happen but something right and beneficial generally, if not always, does. It is a form of help one individual can give another.

I have known a man, with an inoperable brain tumour given numerous sessions of this type of healing, being cured. Another had blocked arteries around the heart, which cleared after numerous sessions over one week. One cancer patient, Eve, was given the strength and inner peace to pass over quickly and quietly. Eve cut the expected six weeks of agony into one week of good-byes to friends and loved ones, and two days of hospitalisation until a dream took her from this life to beyond. This type of healing borders on miracles and cannot be explained. In cases such as these, perhaps we should just accept rather than question or doubt. Miracles of healing for those who are cured and the hope the rest of us receive are mysteries. Why question how they occur when we should probably just be thankful that this method of healing is possible?

Creative Visualisation

Visualisation begins with imagination. Everyone can do it. It is like pretending when we were a child. The important fact about visualisation is that it has the power to affect our body. It is a power of the mind that everyone has and often uses quite naturally. For some it is more pronounced than for others just like some can paint better than others.

Try this little exercise:

- Close your eyes and visualise having a lemon in your hand. Vividly see it. Picture the colour.
- Feel the texture of its skin between your fingers.
- Pretend to smell the lemon.
- Take an imaginary knife and cut the lemon in two.
- Watch the juice run out and feel it cool yet sticky on your skin.
- Now bite into the lemon.

Are you salivating? Did you screw up your face at the thought of biting into the lemon? Did you have any reaction? Everyone I have ever met has had some. This is proof of the connection between visualising in the mind and reaction in the body?

We can use this connection in self-healing.

When we visualize, it is much like creating our own movie in our own mind. Have you ever read a book and then seen the movie and been disappointed? It is simply because our own imagination colours our thoughts and the film is the product of the director's imagination. We all think differently. When we create our own visualisation, we are completely in tune with ourselves. Being our own work makes it extra powerful. The scenes are much more vivid just like our imagined version of the book.

Creating a health visualisation teaches the body how to get well. Continual repetition sets the goal into becoming real. Repetition gives the goal power to manifest it in the physical.

Here are the ingredients to preparing for effective visualisation-

- ALWAYS practice in a QUIET PLACE where you will not be disturbed.
- Soft music may help but silence could be better.
- Avoid bright or flashing lights and uneven or extreme temperatures. These may distract you from your visualisation as you lose concentration from the mental when the physical discomfort intrudes.
- Turn off the mobile.

Recipe: Feel, See, and Hear

- Begin by relaxing and breathing gently. This may take a few minutes. Then begin the visualisation.

STEP 1

- Spend a moment making a picture of your illness. This may be small, black dots floating around your body if you have a virus, a lump of black if there is a growth or tumour or just layers of fat if you are obese. Once you have the picture move on. Do not dwell on the image you are trying to clear. Dwelling on it focuses the energy onto the unwanted condition you are trying to change.

STEP 2

- Picture your illness going. Imagine either an absence of black dots, the lump shrinking, or the layers of fat dissolving. The picture in Step 2 must fix the problem in Step 1.

STEP 3

- Picture your illness gone. This is the ultimate goal. Look where the problem was and notice it gone. You are perfectly healthy, free of the need to smoke, or free of whatever condition previously troubled you.

STEP 4

- Vividly picture yourself well. Imagine all the things you can do when well. Vivid images are best. The brighter and happier and more excited the better. The more energy you give this step the more positive power you create for the healing. Listen to the associated sounds and smell the smells. Live the part. Above all, get in touch with the feeling of being well.

STEP 5

- Hold this image in your mind continually colouring it with emotions of happiness, excitement, joy, and thanks.

Repeat the exercise depending on need. One to three times per day for 21 or 30 days will be enough for many complaints. Long term and serious conditions naturally take longer to clear. Let your inner feeling be your guide. Holding the image (step 5) for 3 to 5 minutes is generally sufficient.

Specific Recipe example—

Take whatever seems logical in curing your complaint. If you are having money problems and wanting to cure a lean purse then you could picture the lack in the form of an empty purse for step 1. Follow in Step 2 as coins or notes floating in and stuffing the purse full.

WARNING: If your problem is your boss, ex-spouse or some other disliked individual, do not imagine them being harmed. The Law of Karma clearly states that you cannot harm others without also drawing it upon yourselves. There is truth in the words of the ancients. What goes around, comes around. What we sow, we reap. It is part of universal law just as creative visualisations use universal law for healing. We cannot abuse the power without hurting ourselves. Actually the explanation is simple. Thoughts cause a vibration. Whatever thoughts are focused are magnetised and will draw back like vibrations that will manifest as circumstances and experiences or things to the thinker.

You cannot overdose on this. My father practiced this while he was waiting for by-pass surgery. All he was physically capable of doing after his massive heart attack was healing meditations. He would do one on waking, one after breakfast, another after morning tea, one after lunch, one after afternoon tea, one after his evening meal, and one following every time he work during the night. He was waiting for a triple by-pass but by the time his operation was performed one artery had healed mysteriously on its own and the damage was not as bad as doctors first thought.

Recipe: Cleansing Breath

- Begin by slowly breathing out three times and letting yourself relax.
- Imagine yourself out on a snow covered mountain-top.

- Breathe in the fresh cool air. As you breathe in the air, notice that it is crisp and clear. Hold the breath within you, then slowly breathe out your stale air.
- Let the golden light from the sun above you become the air you are breathing in. It flows in through your nose, down to the lungs and sits in your solar plexus. While you gently, without strain, hold your breath, feel the light as it gathers strength and transforms any stress into relaxation, any illness into health. As you breathe out gently, the golden light radiates throughout your body.
- Continue to breathe in the golden light to your solar plexus. Breathe out the negativity, any tension you may have, and the illness that the golden light has transformed. The golden light will carry and transform until you feel clear of the condition and cleansed throughout your whole body.
- 3 to 10 breaths should be sufficient.

It may take some practice to co-ordinate the breaths and the visualisation. Once this technique is mastered it can be practiced anywhere whenever the need arises. Life is forever bringing situations that we can turn to our advantage. Harbouring guilt, resentment, and anger stifles our life by draining our energies. It lets us limit ourselves and this has an effect on our health. Practicing this visualisation can reverse the process.

The Chakras and Colour

Chakras are energy centres of the body that run just in front of the spine from the crown of the head down to the tailbone. There is some difference among consciousness teachers about their exact location, colour and qualities. When the energy centres are aligned and in balance, we have quality of life. If they are out of balance illness and disruptions can occur. When blockages in the energy flows are released, they return to balance. This can be done with meditation, crystals, Reiki and spiritual healing.

Study of chakras is quite fascinating, as they have been attributed to having the ability to affect all the different aspects of our lives. This is a grey area where body, mind, and soul overlap. Here explanations are difficult because science and religion meet. Although all agree, they also differ slightly.

At times the centres are depleted or overcharged and then our life is out of balance. When this happens we become ill. In fact, the balance is disrupted before we actually become physically ill. Bringing these centres back into balance, we should then heal the body of the illness. Getting rid of blocked energies lets the body return to perfect balance. One way of returning our energy body back to balance is through creative visualisation or Chakras meditation.

The best time to do the following meditation is early in the mornings to set your day in the right vibration and you in a positive frame of mind. It will take some time to become proficient but once mastered, it takes about ten minutes. This visualisation should not be done immediately after a heavy meal.

There is a slight variation between consciousness teachers about the exact place, colour or quality of each chakra. Accept what feels right for you.

Recipe: The Rainbow of Life

- Begin in a quiet time and place, without disturbance, where you will find peace.
- Sit cross-legged or comfortably on a chair keeping your back straight.
- Breathe out slowly and breathe in fresh clean air.
- Breathe out while seeing in your mind's eye that your body is cleansing.

- Breathe out and imagine the mind/spirit being cleansed.
- Imagine you are in a quiet place in nature and the sun is above you. The golden/white rays of the sun are slowly relaxing your body.
- Begin with the crown of your head and feel the rays of the sun go in and through your head. As the light and warmth enters, your brain and forehead relax releasing all the tension.
- Let the warmth and the rays of light relax the little muscles around your eyes and past your ears to chin. Relax your cheeks and let your jaw drop slightly. All your face and head are now relaxed all the way to the end of every hair.
- Begin in the medulla oblongata or cave at the back of your head. Let the rays of the sunlight in, and relax. Let the warmth of the sun relax your back, especially the two rows of muscles on either side of your spine. Let the relaxation flow down your shoulders, upper arms, forearms, hands, and into your fingers all the way to the tips of each nail.
- Go back to the shoulders. Allow the flow of light, warmth, and relaxation down the front of your body entering every inner organ.
- Your lungs fill with warmth and relax. Your heart, liver, stomach, and spleen fill with warmth and relax. Relax the digestive system, the reproductive system, and your elimination organs. Let the sunlight relax your thighs, calves and down into the foot until it has reached all the way to the tips of every toenail.
- With your body totally relaxed, imagine a tunnel of sunlight going through the crown of your head, down the centre of your body, along your spine to the base of the spine.
- Now take your consciousness to the base of your spine. This is the first, base, or root chakra. It vibrates with the red energy and the sound of middle C or doe. Associated with the element of earth, this is the seat of fears and insecurity. Bring in the light from the sun and balance your root chakra. See the wheel of swirling red energy at the base of your spine in your mind's eye, and know it is clear and open.

- Move your consciousness gently up to the area behind your navel. This is your second or spleen chakra. Associated with the element water, it is orange and the sound of "D". As the seat of our reproductive organs, it also holds quality of life, creativity, vitality, and youth. Bring in the light from the sun and balance your second chakra as the orange energy wheel spins and opens.

- Gently move your consciousness to the third energy centre at your solar plexus. The colour is yellow, the sound "E", and the element fire. It is the seat of our emotions and personal feelings. The inner organs of digestion are involved with this energy centre. This explains why hunger is better regulated once we settle our emotional problems. Focusing here will also settle nervous butterflies and stress related stomach ulcers. Physically your personal power lies here, as do the qualities of faith, joy, and hope. Let in the warmth and sunlight into your third chakra. Watch the yellow energy wheel spin and the open to the goodness of the universe.

- Shift your consciousness to your heart centre in the middle of your chest. The colour of the vibration is green and its sound "F". This is linked to the element of air and the gatekeeper of higher levels. Our heart is the centre in which we hold our feelings, our love for other people, and our love for self. Also, our love for Mother Earth. Let in the unconditional love of the universe by letting in the rays of light from the sun, and balance the aspects of receiving and giving within your life. Within your heart are your qualities of compassion, sincerity, loyalty, and forgiveness. Disruptions in this chakra will let jealousy show up. Let in the light from the sun and the unconditional love of the Most High source of Love. Bring in the balance as the wheel of green energy spins and your heart chakra opens.

- Raise your consciousness to your throat. This is the seat for your fifth chakra. Its colour is blue and the sound is "G". This is your centre for communications and self-expression in all areas of life. This is also where you release judgment. Focusing on the blue light will let you acquire the choice of correct words to properly express yourself while and allowing others their expression. The qualities of honesty and power, dignity and pride are located here. This is the gateway to your psychic and spiritual levels. Let in the light from the sun as the wheel of blue energy turns, balances, and opens.

- Gently move your consciousness to the centre of your forehead or third eye. The colour of the third-eye chakra is indigo and the sound "A". This is the place within your body for psychic and mental development. It is the seat of vision and of your destiny. Whatever you can see here, you can manifest into your life. Imagination is under the control of your sixth chakra. Qualities of energy, beauty, and radiance resonate here. Also happiness and generosity. Through imagination and idealization, you can plan how to better this world. Let in the light from the sun, and balance this area of your life. As the wheel of indigo energy spins, open yourself to the beauty of the universe.

- Move your consciousness to the crown of the head. Here is your seventh chakra. This is violet in colour and associated with the sound "B". It is the area of cosmic energy and soul evolution. Here we hold our vision of what the Sacred Energy of the Universe (God) is. It is the gateway to our higher self. The qualities of inspiration and idealization come together with divine understanding within this vibration. Balance your crown chakra by bringing in the light from above. As the wheel of violet energy spins and opens, you find yourself in complete balance.

- All the chakras are now balanced and in line. The energy is beginning to rise from your base chakra, through all the energy centres, and flows out your top chakra at the crown of the head. Feel the energy as it drops or flows down the outside of your body rejoining at the base. All the energy centres are open and balanced. The energy is flowing like

> a river up through the centre of your body, and back down the outside in a never-ending flow. The vibrations are lifted and you feel vibrant. This increased energy will remain with you throughout this day and the next.
> - Slowly return your consciousness to this world, this time, and this place. Become aware of your physical body and gently return to this reality, refreshed and at peace.

There is a powerful visualisation which can be done on special occasions only. Either New Year, Easter or on your birthday is a good time. Have someone read it slowly to you, giving you time to imagine the scenery. Or read the exercise onto a tape while keeping your voice soothing and quiet, and possibly adding some quiet, peaceful meditation music. Remember to make sure you are in perfect surroundings and will not be disturbed. Begin with the precursor recipes of Consciousness Relaxation or the Cleansing Breath to ensure you are relaxed before starting.

Recipe: Regeneration

- Imagine yourself as a seed below the ground. You are in complete darkness. Feel the ground as it restricts you while you are safe in your little, cocoon-like shell.
- A drop of pure water reaches you from above. This is the magic ingredient, which softens the earth around you. It softens the outer casing of your shell and you begin to swell.
- Grow up towards the source from which the life giving water has come. Reach down into the earth for nourishment. Leave the tensions, stress, negative thoughts, and old worn out ideas, beliefs, and habits. They remain in the Earth while you become new.
- Break through the surface into the sunlight. Feel the warmth of the sunlight as it flows through every cell of your existence. It relaxes and heals as it goes. It cleanses and rejuvenates.

- Feel the drops of rain that fall. They swell your heart. Give you strength and energy.
- Feel the cool of the night as it gives you guidance and direction, peace, and the time to look at the direction of your life. The new day gives you the freshness and enthusiasm to step forward with pride, strength, and inner conviction.
- You blossom into beauty and spread the seeds of your dreams. With their emergence float free and be released.
- You become a bird. Fly free and effortless back to your body bringing with you the inner strength and energy. Feel yourself cleansed and at peace.
- Slowly return to the present time and place, feeling refreshed.

Healing with Colours

Colour is a vibration between light and darkness. We see different colours according to their wavelength. Colours also have different temperatures and their sounds resonate in harmony. The colour red has the longest wavelength and the slowest vibration. Violet is the opposite. Between red and violet is the whole rainbow of colour.

Red is a warm colour, a dense feeling and burns to touch. Blue is cool and open. Green is a neutral colour.

Light is part of our external environment. Each day has separate colours that many are not even aware of. The morning is white golden light and as the day wears on it becomes orange and the sunset turns red. Neon lights tend to excite us, as do the shop lights, while candlelight has a calming effect.

We can heal with colours by imagining ourselves bathed in a particular colour. For asthma, insomnia and tension use blue light. Lethargy and tiredness can be cured with reds. Anxiety and aggression is depleted with pinks. In fact just looking at a sheet of soft pink cardboard for 5 to

10 minutes will absorb anger. Weightlifters are able to lift less weight in a room coloured with soft pastel colours, especially pink. Red and black in combination are erotic and stimulating colours.

Health problems can be helped with the colour of the corresponding chakra or energy centre. Concentrating on the colour blue can cure a hoarse throat. For lung and heart conditions, work with the colours of pink and green. Meditating on indigo can cause a headache if the colour is in excess. I personally found that in the beginning I always used white light because it contains all colours and the body takes whichever vibration it needs.

Mastery over Mind

Our mind is a powerful instrument. Whatever happens to us during our whole life is sifted through our minds and so we form opinions and beliefs according to what we see. Our mind can be either our best friend or our worst enemy. When it works with us to help us achieve our goals, it is our best friends. When we cannot sleep at night because of nightmares, when we are paralysed from fears and held back from enjoying ourselves, the mind is our worst enemy.

We have the power of choice over our thoughts! If you think this is not so let me tell you it is. Maybe no one has ever told you before? No one has probably explained about the mind and thoughts throughout your whole formal schooling. However, you have probably been told to think!

The mind has a constant flow of thoughts going through it. Someone once estimated in excess of 10,000 thoughts per day. How often is the same thought repeated? How often is one followed so closely by another that we feel we are thinking many at once? Is it any wonder if our lives are not going exactly as we choose? Let us be realistic—often it is quite overwhelming. We have problems and become stressed.

We can think no further or we get lost in the never-ending spiral of repeated thoughts.

Anyone can stop this cycle and become master over mind once they are taught how. We can trick the mind into becoming like a broken record. Before we had CDs and cassette tapes, we had records. A tiny needle would run along the spiral of groves to give us the music to listen or dance to. If the needle were bumped, it would sometimes cut the grove and then run over the same few words repeatedly. This is where the saying of a broken record came from. The mind can do this as well. Have you noticed, when you have a problem you are plagued with the same few thoughts focusing on the problem? The mind can drive us into despair. We become crazy with this never changing repetition. The answer generally lies just below this layer of confusion but we cannot reach it. We become frustrated and angry. Driven far enough, we are said to lose our mind. This is only losing control—control over your own thoughts and your mind.

There is a trick to fixing this problem. It is to reach the area of mind where the answers lurk. We use the broken record technique on the mind. Each of us is the master of our own mind, or at least we can be if we choose. We are the thinkers. We are boss and so we choose to give the conscious mind a broken record to exist in, while we go beyond into the sub-conscious. This technique lets the crazy thoughts disappear from the mind because one specific word or sentence continually overruns them.

Recipe: Broken Record (Mantra Method)

- Repeat one positive, beneficial word over and over in your mind.

The word should be something constructive and positive because words have and energy of themselves as they paint pictures of their meanings into our minds. This is why we find we fail ourselves whenever we plan to sabotage someone else. And why the saying 'we reap what we sow' is a natural law.

Peace. Love. Life. I am. These words create healing vibrations. The Broken Record recipe, using these positive words puts your body in a higher vibration and will take your mind into a peaceful healing state.

Use this technique if you wake in the small hours of the morning and are plagued by the "what if . . ." Stop the flow from one possible bad situation to the next.

Use this technique if there is a problem that does not seem to have a solution. Instead of focusing on the problem, the mind is distracted and the answer will be given the opportunity to emerge when you are relaxed. Before beginning the repetitions, decide that you are seeing a solution. Practice this technique and the answer may just suddenly present itself. This may happen the very first time that you try it. It may not happen in a week of practicing this exercise twice daily. It may just pop in as an idea unexpectedly while you are doing something completely unrelated. You may see a movie or have a visitor who suddenly talks about someone else with a similar problem and you will get your answer. It may even come as a dream. The mind works in mysterious ways and the possibilities are endless. When we open our mind and have chosen with conviction, barriers are overcome and we open the gates for possible miracles to occur. Just as we keep people away by locking the door to our house, so we can mentally close the door to our needs and wants without realising it. Opening the mind is the greatest step any person can make, especially a person seeking healing.

The Three Levels of Mind

It is important to understand the workings of the mind to control it and harness its power for healing or for deliberately creating a desired outcome.

The mind is actually on three levels. If I am asked draw the mind, I draw an iceberg. The part looking out of the water is like the conscious mind. The mind we are aware of. It is the place where we do our thinking. It is also the part that used to program the remaining mind, much like filling in information into a computer screen. It functions and has incredible uses.

The sub-conscious mind is like the nine-tenths of the iceberg that remains underwater. It is the part, which stops us from falling out of bed at night. It controls our functions, keeps us breathing without us having to think about it. This mind sends hormones into our bodies. It tells us to remove our hand when we put it on the hotplate and registers the pain of our burn.

The sub-conscious mind also holds our beliefs and attitudes. It holds the answers to our problems and can be reached when we know how. Another function of the sub-conscious mind is to connect to the super-conscious mind that is the universal mind or the source of divine intelligence. When we get an inspiration, it is the sub-conscious mind that brings the ideas, music, feelings, or whatever from the universal Source of Divine Intelligence. From the sub-conscious it comes into our conscious, thinking mind. When there is a health problem and we wish to plug into this state of mind, we are reaching the natural healing state previously mentioned in this book.

Fears and Barriers

Fears and mental barriers are nothing but thoughts have been accepted as real. A belief is only a set of thought that are thought of habitually until they seem real because no thoughts to the contrary readily exist. Individuals hold themselves back with unfounded fears and imaginary barriers to their health, wealth and happiness.

Granted, some fears are necessary to our survival and natural. We fear walking across a busy city street against the lights in case we instantly meet our maker. We do not disturb poisonous snakes or swim in shark infested waters or let our children play on the beach with crocodiles. These are natural fears that protect our existence but so often, we fear people and situations that will not harm us.

Often stress is the result of unnecessary fears. We play games in our minds and let the fears run free and develop. A client of mine stressed over the following situation. He worried and worried about a work contract that he thought might be in danger of collapsing. If the contract was cancelled he may be terminated then not be able to pay his mortgage commitments. He worried even though all was fine and he had not even been given the indication of a problem. Had a problem occurred he still would have had the possibility of work elsewhere to meet his financial obligations. Yet he worried and stressed. I explained that assuming the absolute worst possible situation, he was still alive, could camp with family and friends and would still not starve to death. The level of his fear was unreasonable and unfounded. Putting the whole situation in context allowed him to let go of his fears and his stress disappeared.

What unnecessary fears or imagined dragons are you feeding in your life?

Human are funny creatures. We have a mind and misuse it when we don't understand the inner workings. Perhaps this is because no-one is ever taught the proper use of the most powerful instrument for creating life that we own.

We let our minds threaten us through possible not probable fears. When we let fears and mental barriers paralyse us, we are letting the negative thoughts of the mind control our lives. Through this error in judgement we are actually LETTING our mind be our own worst enemy.

When you learn to control your negative thoughts, you will have a weapon to keep all your fears in check, and force your mind to work for you. That is why you have a mind—so you can think and analyse, you can weigh up your choices in any situation or circumstances, and then choose the best alternative. The mechanism of mind should be working FOR YOU.

The Common fears

There are 7 common fears that we all harbour to some degree or another. These are the fears of—

- Poverty—not having enough food, work or money
- Criticism—not being good enough, what others will think, social standing
- loss of love—not being liked, not being worthy, the end of relationships
- ill health—getting a disease or not being able to keep up
- change—being unable to adapt to the ever changing situations and circumstances
- old age—losing the beauty, shape and capabilities of the body, not keeping up and
- death—the biggest fear. This fear is often disguised as fearing ends and conclusions such as death of relationships, death of job, death of body.

Fears are more difficult and insidious that they first appear because they have two components—a positive and a negative. Fear of change can manifest as the fear of failure and/or the fear of success. You have the power to cut most of these fears down to size by grasping power over your own mind. By thinking positive thoughts and rationalising fears, you can be much happier and calm. When you focus on the positive dreams and desires rather than the negative possibilities, you are using your mind as a valuable ally and fears will disappear. You will be denying them power over you. Even the big one—fear of death—will be eliminated later in this book. Meanwhile there are some easy recipes for controlling stress and fears that you might like to try.

Recipe: Rating the Problem

- Begin by establishing a scale from 0 to 10.
- Assume 10 is 100%—chance of death—the worst that can happen at any point in time. Use the idea that at death you cannot continue in this life at all. (Even if you believe in reincarnation, you will not return to this exact time, family, and physical situation so death has a finality.)
- Now think of the fear or problem.
- Rate it along the scale of 1 to 10. Rate the situation you are in right now, NOT WHAT IT MAY DEVELOP INTO.
- Realise that few situations in life are actual 10s yet we create unnecessary stress by imagining the worst.
- Recognising the problem as less than all encompassing.
- Open your mind to possibilities.
- Then the mental lockdown or paralysis caused by the fear disappears.

Once you control your fears, anything is possible—almost anything. I control my thoughts but am still reluctant to go bungee jumping, sky-diving or experimenting with drugs. Extreme sports are not my thing and harmful activities should be avoided anyway.

In a single step, controlling fears is about controlling negative thoughts.

Negative Thoughts

Eliminating negative thoughts is an important part of controlling the mind. It is essential when faced with a terminal disease or chronic complaint. When we have a life-threatening situation, fears are natural, and the mind continues to paint worst scenario pictures that will feed the illness. This is particularly the case for cancers. A body vibrating with fears held in the mind will deteriorate quicker than one holding the healing vibrations of peace. It is impossible to feel at peace and have hope for the future when our mind is running through a series of negative thoughts building panic.

Panic is just a series of individual ultra-negative thoughts, which come quickly in what seems more of a flood than a stream. When you realise that your mind can only think one thought at a time, you have the key to the solution. Once you learn to control one negative thought, you can control any thought at any time. You are then free to find the inner peace so beneficial to healing.

Exterminate Negative Thoughts

A negative thought can only harm you while you hold it in your mind and let fear build. Consider a moment how every person can walk along a six-foot long plank lying on the ground. Most people can walk along that plank if it was even elevated a few inches off the ground. Once the same plank is placed at the top rung between two stepladders, the fear of possible damage to life and limb through a fall would prohibit most of us from walking along that same plank. Fears are only negative thoughts and can harm us once we acknowledge their existence. In this case the fear is quite legitimate and your mind is protecting you from danger but often fears are unfounded. The doctor told Sharon she was gluten sensitive and should eliminate bread from her diet but Sharon thinks she can't give up her sandwiches. She feels horrible but can't imagine being able to stick to any diet. Imagining that being able to adhere to an eating plan is simply a negative thought which can be overcome. Let's look at ways to exterminate negative thoughts and limitations.

Recipe: Exterminate Negatives #1—Delete or Cancel

- As soon as you are aware you are thinking a negative thought, imagine it on a computer screen and press the delete or cancel button.
- You can thank the idea for coming to you but then delete it without emotion.

In this age of computers, mobiles and tablets, most people are aware of the effect of the Delete Key. A deleted negative thought is powerless because it no longer exists. Something that does not exist cannot cause harm. And it certainly cannot attract its mates to grow into minor anxiety. Once deleted the negative cannot deplete energy. As your energy remains intact, you give yourself the chance to be or stay happy.

Do you realise that situations affect us more when we are directly involved. If a stranger's car has a flat tyre, we feel little emotion compared to us having the flat tyre. If you could simply detach from the situation, the negative emotion would dissolve and the negative thoughts disappear. It could even become an adventure, a new learning experience or a challenge to overcome. That would turn the whole situation into a therapy session building self-esteem. Here is a recipe to learn to detach from a negative situation.

Recipe: Exterminate Negatives #2—Watch it

- Play the innocent bystander.
- Mentally note that you had a negative thought.
- Watch the thought as if it were separate from you.
- Thank it for emerging or coming and then send it away
- Attach no emotion to the whole experience.

This is a cold scientific type of control. It is standing back from the situation realising that you and your thoughts are separate identities. When we have a bad thought it may make us feel bad but it does not mean we are bad. We have the power to choose to retain the thought, develop it, or reject it but we are not the thought itself.

Recipe: Exterminate Negatives #3—The 100% Switch

- As soon as you realise you are having a negative thought immediately think the opposite.
- Totally become immersed in the desired outcome.

Here is an example of the switch. It goes like this: 'I am not going to recover this time . . .' negative . . . switch . . . 'I am going to recover as I have many times before—I am vibrantly healthy and feel great!' At this point, feel the success, imagine it so strongly like it was real and has already happened to you. The power of your emotions gives power to your thoughts. The change from negative to positive builds rather than depletes your energy. You literally feel the difference. As you are in control of your thoughts, you are also in control of your feelings and you recognise your own power.

Recipe: Exterminate Negatives #4—Clown Around

- As soon as you become conscious of a negative thought exaggerate it into the ridiculous.

Alternately,

- If it will be funny in hindsight, see that funny side now by enhancing the situation.

Here is an example of clowning around to kill a negative thought. Imagine if your temperature has risen one degree above where you should be. When your mind begins to paint pictures of your health being a problem, play along with it. Imagine yourself going up in temperature until you reach 100degrees C. Imagine blowing steam out of your ears and being bright red.

Your mind will instantly realise this is impossible and the thread of the tempting worry story that you would have been part of has disappeared. The worry has suddenly lost its power over you. Negatives only have power over us when we let them. We give our little fears the power to literally grow into nightmares.

Obsessive thoughts—negatives in the heavy duty version

Obsessive thoughts are those that keep recurring. They persist and are resistant to normal methods of elimination. For them, we use a creative visualisation. They are special and require special attention.

Recipe: Exterminate Negatives #5—The Clear Path

- Imagine that you are out in nature.
- Picture before you, a path to a tree. This path is strewn with rocks. These rocks represent your recurring thoughts.
- Walk towards the tree and shift all the rocks out of your way as you go. Whichever method you use to destroy the rocks is up to you. I like to explode them into nothingness.
- When you reach the tree simply turn around and walk back to where you began. You can now walk on a straight clear path.
- Focus on the feeling of freedom and enthusiasm as your path ahead is clear.

The clear path visualisation may have to be done a second time if the thoughts are particularly obsessive or if they have been occurring for a particularly long time.

Recipe: Exterminate Negatives #6—Magic Fire

- Imagine yourself writing the unwanted recurring idea, thought, or fear onto a piece of paper.
- In your imagination, build a fire in front of you and let it get white hot.
- The fire is cleansing and magic. Gently put the paper you have just written on into the fire. You will not burn your hand if you accidentally touch the flame.
- As the fire eats the paper, it will eliminate the thought or idea you are also cleansing from your life.

Continual Persistence

Using these exercises to rid the mind of negative thoughts will need to go on as often as the negative thoughts occur. You now have some weapons to help you control your mind and thus control the waking nightmares but be patient with yourself as you practice. You may have spent your whole life thinking in a particular way so you may not be able to change overnight. Work at it with persistence. Imagine the power of a drop of water dripping constantly on a rock. It literally wears the hardest rock away. In the same way you can learn to control your thinking.

As you change your thoughts and change your attitude of life, life will reflect a happier healthier you. This is because thoughts have energy and raising the level of thoughts will also raise your spirits.

In time, you will find your attitude has changed and few negatives arise. Negative thoughts are sneaky little devils so be aware when they sneak back in. You will probably never stop them altogether but that is OK. You are in control. You have personal power and can get rid of them rather than let them harm the quality of your life.

For people who have not been exposed to mind-work before, I recommend beginning with a Four-Week Positive Diet. This means monitoring your thoughts for a period of four weeks and concentrating on eliminating destructive negative thoughts for that period. After four weeks, you will have trained yourself to think in a positive mindset.

One note of warning: Sometimes positives come through negatives. I have heard of a number of people who have had a small accident. Each then visited the doctor because of an uneasiness of mind, and was diagnosed with high blood pressure or diabetes, which needed immediate attention. When I first began this process, I had three health incidents on which I wanted an expert opinion, in one week. The doctor I had at that time did not understand and thought I was a hypochondriac. I changed doctors.

Recipe: Cleansing the Mind

- Stand or sit straight.
- Take the fingers from your dominant hand and touch the forehead. This is the energy centre of your psyche. Psyche may sound ominous but literally means of mind and spirit.
- Trace out three small clock-wise circles in the centre of the forehead to build energy.
- Take the fingers of your other hand to your forehead. While saying the words, either aloud or silently in your mind, "I now cleans my body", slowly sweep the hands down the centre of your body. Imagine those fingers reaching through your whole body and sweeping away all the debris that has accumulated there.
- Shake your hands to rid yourself of any accumulation before continuing.
- Put the hands just below the chin and sweep the hands up the face around the top of the head down to the back of the neck while saying, "I now cleanse my mind and soul".
- Shake your hands twice.

You can add the Infinite Divine Source of Power to the exercise.

"In the name of the Power of the Universe I cleanse my body, and my mind and soul".

Substitute the Power of the Universe with God, or whatever name you use for your most Holy and Divine Source. If in your heart of hearts you know that no divine being exists, just go through the actions.

Attitude and Beliefs

Attitudes, values and beliefs are only a series of thoughts we keep thinking about particular subjects, people or ideas. They have been taught to us just as carefully as a computer gets programmed. The older generation was taught by parents and teachers. The younger among us have been increasingly taught by media, advertising and the environment. We learn how and what to think, what opinions to have, and judge what is good and right accordingly. The shoes to wear are Nike. Coca-Cola is the real thing. Smoking is cool. Marijuana doesn't harm the brain. I hate vegetables.

Society looks at a growing crime rate and the lack of respect many teenagers have for their parents, other people and things in general yet few teenagers have not played violent computer games, been absorbed in the virtual world or been part of some cyber group. If thoughts program your brain and visualisation can create your future, why would you immerse yourself in violence and war for fun?

What and where we are in life is the product of our choices and those depend on our values, ideas and beliefs. Everyone is a product of his or her thoughts. If you believe, education is useless, you will avoid school. On the other hand, if you know or have been taught that education is valuable and nothing worthwhile is possible without qualifications, you will keep happily studying for years. Either path is right. SO LONG as you are acting consistently with your thoughts, you will feel happy.

Thoughts, attitude and beliefs guide the choices we make and the choices create our circumstances and experiences. If your life is not giving you the experiences and circumstances, people and places you think you would like, change your thoughts. If you are not happy with your life, particularly with your state of health, you have the power to change it through the power of your mind and choice of thoughts.

Perhaps I can live without sugar or I can eat vegetables or maybe I can survive on less food . . . If I can change my choices, perhaps I can get my slim body back? Maybe I can fit daily walks into my timetable?

Our choice of thoughts will set our attitude. We can learn to be our own best friend by choosing to entertain only beneficial thoughts but first we have to know what beliefs we really do have.

Recipe: Thought and Belief Analysis part 1

- Begin with a blank piece of paper.
- Head it with the title My thoughts about my health.
- Write at least 20 facts you believe about your health.

These may be anything like the following:

- I heal quickly.
- I have a high pain threshold.
- I have weak lungs.
- I am grossly unfit.

The purpose of the exercise is to expose any deep unconscious beliefs that may be producing your problems or could be hindering your healing process. Once these thoughts are exposed, they need to be eliminated.

Recipe: Thought and Belief Analysis part 2

When you have finished your list, take a big bold felt tip pen.

- Put a + sign on any positive ideas and a—sign on the negative ones. (Being positive that you are unfit still deserves a—sign!)
- Rewrite those beliefs with a + sign on a clean page and keep them. These are already working to keep you healthy.
- Change any negatives into positives by writing their opposites and then adding them to your page. Example: I haven't the time to exercise becomes I have the time to exercise.
- In a safe place, burn the old page and watch your previous negatives transform into ash. Pick up the ash and discard it.
- Use the positive list as a daily reminder sheet and read it twice daily for a month. After that time the belief will be programmed into your brain.

You have now gotten rid of the negative thought patterns. The thoughts have flowed into the universe and are released from your world in the form of energy. You have given them away and set yourself free. The warmth of the flames and any smoke are evidence of their flowing out and you are cleansed.

You do not need to limit these processes to just analyzing your thoughts about health. Money, career, relationships, social position or any area of life that is a challenge or where you would like improvement can be worked on with this technique. Try it and have fun. The object is to improve your life and your happiness.

Transforming Beliefs

This recipe is similar to the one above and is also in two parts. Part A emphasises the positive. Part B dissolves any power of negatives.

Recipe: Part A—Increasing the Positive Power

- Write at the top of a paper in bold letters the words, 'I deserve to be healthy'.
- Note your reaction, write down the thought that comes in
- Then write the words 'Thank you'.
- Repeat these steps at least 20 to 25 times.

The first five thoughts generally come easily. After a while you will tend to repeat those first few and wonder if that is all you believe but then, your mind will reach deeper into your more deep-seated and hidden beliefs and the surprises will begin.

Recipe: Part B—Decreasing the Negative Power

- Write either 'I thought my health was a barrier to . . . and fill in the blank or' My health limits me because . . . . and fill in the blanks.
- After your answer, write the words: 'Thank you. I now dissolve that thought.'
- Write the whole series at least 20 to 25 times. Remember the technique from Part A that deep-seated thoughts take some effort to discover. I tend to concentrate a little longer on the negatives to root them out.

Here is a real-life example. Jerry began his list:

- *'My health limits me because I have a bad heart. Thank you, I now dissolve that thought.'*
- *'My health limits me because my nerves are shot. Thank you, I now dissolve that thought.'*

And so on. The list went on and on and I thought he would never stop. Finally he got silence. Then his mind must have realised that life is not all bad and flipped into the positive. He rarely has had a negative thought about his health since.

No thought or belief you have is wrong. It came from somewhere and is leading you somewhere. If the belief is not beneficial to where you want to go, you have the power to change it. Getting hung up on why you have the belief will not progress you into a better place. To change your belief you have to actively build a new belief and we have a recipe for that too.

Recipe: Building New Beliefs

- Decide on a new belief that will enhance your life—one that will improve or maintain vibrant health.
- Spend 3-5 minutes daily for 21 or 30 days reprogramming your thinking and affirming the truth of the statement. Feel it true within yourself. Say the words repeatedly. When your mind wanders off and you begin to think of tonight's movie or last night's dinner, just refocus on the new belief.

Holding the new belief and repeating it, feeling it, living it in your mind, will make the mind believe it.

Remember that your statement must be positive, in the present tense and not detrimental to another.

It may read something like the following:

- *'I am a miracle of creation and naturally deserving of all the good things life has to offer.'*
- *'My body is naturally healing itself through its inbuilt life-force'.*
- *'I am well. I am well. I am well, fit and vibrantly healthy. I am well. I am.'*

Self-talk

Self-talk is the inner conversation that continues in our mind. It continually programs our subconscious and sets up belief systems that we often are not even aware of.

Whether we have a health problem and are trying to return to a state of well-being or are healthy and trying to maintain this, our self-talk about health matters are important because it reacts immediately setting attitude and beliefs in motion. Someone will mention that a new virus has emerged. Immediately our self-talk reacts. Either we tell ourselves: "Watch out" and go into a spiral imagining our next illness or we may tell ourselves "I am immune. I am always healthy."

Recipe: Self-talk Watchdog

- Put a watchdog into your mind to discover the content of your self-talk. If it not consistent with health and healing, CHANGE THE BELIEF.
- Build the new, beneficial opinion by affirming it or repeating it.

Acceptance

Life is not perfect. If everything were always perfect, no-one would not appreciate it. This is because we learn and grow by our mistakes and the mind craves stimulation to keep it active and working properly just as the body requires movement.

When life is not perfect a good coping mechanism is acceptance. Sometimes acceptance is the only option. Suppose you had a leg amputated because of injuries sustained in a car-crash, All the wishing, hoping, praying, and healing will not put that leg back. A good dose of acceptance would be a step forward. Acceptance may lead to the point of replacing the leg with prosthesis. At times, the healing process starts with acceptance. Once we accept a condition or problem, we can step forward. While we do not believe we have a problem, we will not take any steps towards seeking a cure, no matter what others say. We live on happily in a state of ignorance.

Recipe: Contemplate the Prayer of Serenity

Contemplating and focusing on the following prayer has helped countless people accept their situation and find a way to improve it.

God, grant me the serenity
To accept the things I cannot change,
Courage to change the things I can
And wisdom to know the difference.

Sometimes we have progressed so far but cannot see our achievements because we are focused on struggle. Patting ourselves on the back for achievements is also part of acceptance.

Recipe: Acknowledge your success

- Spend some time acknowledging yourself for what you have already accomplished.
- Look back to where you began and pat yourself on the back for your progress

When you acknowledge your progress it gives a boost to your ego and enhances positive healing energies. Even little progress should be celebrated. If you can now walk three steps where last week you could only sit up in bed, that is a huge leap forward. Congratulating ourselves when we deserve it gives us the strength and motivation to go on. Past successes are the seeds for future greatness. The more energy and emotion that goes into your acknowledgement the more positive energy you send out. By the Law of Attraction that amount will magnify and will come back to you in the form of circumstances and experiences that will let you feel just as good.

Forgiveness

Forgiveness is another strong emotion that can be used for healing. Forgiveness has two aspects—forgiving others and forgiving oneself.

Forgiveness can seem impossible when the deed or misdeed was huge. How can we forgive the person who has raped our child or murdered a loved one? How can we forgive a spouse for misusing our trust?

Before considering how, let's look at why it is beneficial to forgive both ourselves and others. With understanding of why comes the power to decide and to approach the possibility of how.

There are many negative emotions people harbour and carry that can be released by forgiveness. Guilt is one of these. Hurt, disappointment, jealousy, self-pity and a range of others also exist. Dwelling on any of these, holding the thoughts in mind or focusing on the experiences will cause two unpleasant things to occur.

Firstly as you hold them in your mind by thinking about them, they are causing a vibration of suffering in your body. Secondly they are vibrating energy and whatever energy you vibrate will come back to you through the Law of Attraction. Better to release and forgive? This can be a difficult process. I hear you say—"easier said than done" . . . or perhaps "impossible—you don't know how bad this was". As hard as the process may seem, that is how important it is to forgive.

Think about this on an energy level because on a spiritual level we are energy. When we indulge in guilt for something we have done and not forgiven ourselves for, we are holding negative vibrations within our bodies. As we hold the hurt, the vibrations will manifest into the physical as surely as seeds will sprout given water. When we cannot forgive others for something they have done to us, we hold resentments and hatred. While this may be justified according to the extent of the violation done to us, the feelings create a vibration that affects our health destructively. Metaphysical teachers tell us that anger, guilt, and resentments eventually eat away our body by manifesting into diseases which will do the same in the physical. This does not mean that anyone with cancer must automatically have been harbouring guilt. Cancer comes from eating the wrong foods, being contaminated with chemicals, through exposure to radiation or any number of other causes. It can also have been that the disease has manifested from the vibrations held. Just as sure as day follows night, thoughts that are energised and felt as strong emotions in the body, will manifest into experiences, circumstances and events that will cause the same feelings to manifest again. It is law. The universal Law of Creation gives back whatever you ask for—whether you want it or not.

The important point here is to look into the future and towards possible prevention!!! Not EVERY single negative thought will turn into disaster but if you put the ingredients for scrambles eggs together that is what will cook. Using the recipe for the desires you want makes sense. Not doing those same actions—that same recipe for things you don't want is simply the other side of the equation. For this reason, especially for the huge things, it is primarily for our own good.

To regain health, it is wise to eliminate these negative emotions. If they have by chance not caused the complaint then their presence will certainly hinder, not help recovery. So it is important to release and forgiveness is a way of doing that.

To remain healthy we must forgive—others and ourselves.

Advanced Recipe: Love Thy Enemy

This is exactly like Sending Love to a friend except more difficult to perform. Healing relationships can be very rewarding. Long-standing feuds gradually wear us away because they are like a thorn in our side, eventually becoming infected, and a real health problem.

- Simply focus on someone or something you truly love.
- Transfer that love onto the person with whom you have the grievance.

This recipe can be difficult to perform. The difficulty is directly proportionate to the hurt you feel but also to the relief you will get. So while it may be very hard it will also be very rewarding. Do not worry if this does not work in the very first instance. It takes time to learn to feel differently. If you have trouble, imagine the situation surrounded by golden light of forgiveness, the blue light of healing and the pink light of love.

Sometimes we are just incompatible with our enemy and even getting to love does not seem possible so the process needs to be taken one step at a time. Perhaps try just neutralising the situation and releasing him or her to a different place. Let the universe deal with the situation simply forgetting that he or she exists. After some time has passed, it often becomes possible to transform them from a neutral state into a loving one, if you are still worried about it. Often it is just a matter of getting relief and peace to feel good. That is success too because the negative emotions are no longer present.

Recipe: Apologise

An apology is a statement explaining our mistake and is usually expressed with regret. We are seeking forgiveness.

- Apologise to others if you know you have wronged them.
- Accept that the apology clears the problem and feel the freedom

Apologising like this does not have to be done in the physical if this is not possible. The other party may have passed away, moved on or you have simply lost touch. I know I said something particularly hurtful to one schoolmate while in grade 8 and another to a friend in grade 10. These haunted me for quite some time but when I did an absentee apology, I felt better.

Recipe: Absentee Apology

- Replay the scene in your mind's eye, insert your apology, and their forgiveness. Make sure the reliving contains all the emotion of the real thing. Picture the person in front of you and really feel your regret. The mind is such a miraculous mechanism that your message will reach its target on some level.
- Replay the situation a second time and tell yourself how you are remembering yourself apologising.
- Rerun a short version for a third time to teach the mind to recall the apology.
- Once you have apologised you are free of the past.

Perhaps you regret not being fair to yourself. In that case you may choose to have a DMD—deep and meaningful discussion with yourself. Apologise to yourself.

Letting Go

In nature, there is a continual replacement of the old with the new. Within our bodies, there is also this same process—natural regeneration—constant replacement of worn out cells with new ones. Letting go of the old and worn-out is the natural order of things and it is a healthy. Why then do we hang on to people, situations, and ideas that we have outgrown?

If you never cleared the garbage out of your house, it would become uninhabitable. But we clutter our minds with thoughts, ideas, and beliefs that are no longer valid and our lives with people and situations that have grown stale?

One of the reasons for holding on to things is fear. If we are not happy in our job, we hold on for fear of not getting the continual income stream. Why endure misery for 8—10 hours every workday because of negative thoughts about yourselves and your abilities.

Naturally, there is much to consider for major changes in life but without removing the old you cannot let in the new.

Recipe: Cleaning Up

This works on the physical to clear the meta-physical.

- Clear out the car or your desk, cupboards in your kitchen or rearrange your wardrobe.
- Throw out or give away anything you know you are not going to use again.

Creating order in this way and letting go on the physical is a mirror for the mind/spirit. We can then also let go of old ideas. Letting go in one area of life can open the door to also letting go of health problems.

Within this concept, I am not recommending you get rid of your old friends as I speak of worn out relationships. Old true friends will always remain. Sometimes we do not have as much in common with some people as we once had. This is natural growth and development. With those whom we do not see eye to eye anymore, we can simply enjoy fewer contacts. Slowly, as we drift apart from stale acquaintances, we are free to spend more time with new friends.

Cleaning up relationships may help you feel better if you are ill but we especially need loved ones around us when we are not well. Hoe you feel about the people you spend most of your time with is important. If two people are miserable within their present relationship then it may be better that both move on to find happiness elsewhere rather than endure decades sharing a life with someone they do not like. It is not necessary to break up and separate. Often a little work and some love and understanding will mend many problems. People can also co-exist on separate paths without complete separation. I have known couples who have not divorced but continued to happily share the same house for years after their marriage was over.

It is important to take special care of relationships because all people are special and deserve understanding, respect, and love. Even those, with whom we do not agree. Even those who frustrate and annoy us are special. We have a lesson to learn, especially from them. And then there are the real challenges—the people who don't like themselves.

Recipe: Write it Out

This exercise can be done in one of two ways. Either the whole exercise is performed as a visualisation and done in the imagination, or it can be performed in the physical.

- On a piece of paper, write down your innermost feelings, those things that have upset you and why. Putting it down on paper releases the thoughts from the mind. It gives you the chance to clear it out. Let the pain into the words. Put all your feelings, all the emotions, and any hurt onto the paper. Literally, write it out of your system. As the inner feelings you have revealed to yourself are most private, they are not normally for sharing. Precious secrets that should remain private, the words you have physically written on paper are best burnt after you have finished. This ensures that another who may be hurt by them or may misconstrue them will not accidentally find them.

- Set a safe fire and watch the cleansing take place. Watch the words eaten up by the flames. Let them go. Release them into the universe. Unburden yourself and continue your life with an inner peace that comes from knowing that everything is right in your world.
- Touch that peace that comes from release and understanding.

Sometimes we feel more comfortable talking to people. In that case, use the Imaginary Friend recipe rather than the preceding one.

Recipe: The Imaginary Friend

- Go to a private place where you know you will not be disturbed. Sit alone in the park, climb to the top of a mountain, or visit a lonely beach.
- Imagine someone with you. Imagine this person is your best friend and will understand everything you say. You can tell them your innermost secrets. You are at peace, one with this person.
- Tell this special person your problems, why you did what you did. Tell this special person how you felt, what you thought, and share your burdens. This is a form of confessing.
- Let go of any negative feelings that are attached. With your special person, your guide, work out the emotions that are bothering you. Rid yourself of pain by exposing it. This is just

like a wounded and scratched knee will heal quickly when the sunlight and air can get at it. The thoughts released, wrongs forgiven and feelings cleansed cannot haunt your mind, when they are gone.

- If you are confused, imagine this person giving you loving advice, which will help you to release and let go. Possibly, look for a way to make amends.
- Feel the release and freedom once you have finished. Feel the peace and joy that comes from being unburdened. Thank your imaginary friend and guide before he or she disappears.

Please note that this is not a session of reliving the past so you can wallow in the misery. This is therapy to rid you of your guilt and unload your burdens.

Recipe: Letting Go of Anger

- Take a sheet of soft pastel pink paper or cardboard. Pink fabric or wallpaper will also do.
- Stare at the colour. Become one with the colour.
- Then think of the situation or person who has made you angry.
- Imagine them floating within this pink colour. Imagine the situation dissolving as the power of the pink dissolves the cause of the anger. Imagine the person, completely surrounded, within and without, by the colour pink.
- Notice your anger has melted away and you are free.

When a child has a disappointment or hurt, often the tears flow. Crying is a natural human reaction. It defuses the hurt and the process is available to anyone—though often best done in private.

<u>Recipe: Cry</u>

- Cry, weep, sob to get whatever is hurting you out of your system.
- Let the body's built-in drug supply wash out the hurt.

Men sometimes find it difficult to cry because of society's belief that it is a sign of weakness. Crying when we are frustrated or upset releases natural healing chemicals into the bloodstream to calm us down. This is a safety valve against stress build-up.

<u>Recipe: Fight Fire With Fire</u>

- Punch a pillow or other soft object.

Activity burns up chemicals released by anger. Once they are neutralised, they can no longer harm you.

<u>Recipe: Laugh it Off</u>

- Laugh at the source of the anger and deliberately look on the funny side.

Laughter dissolves anger and stress. Eventually, we often see the funny side anyway but laughing shortens the time before this happens. Laughing at others, with others, and at ourselves, is a valuable stress management tool.

<u>Reprogramming the Memory</u>

Previously in this book I offered the knowledge that thoughts and feelings are linked. What we think affects how we feel. When we have been hurt, disappointed, abused, or raped we hold thoughts that make us relive the pain. If we dwell on the pain, it will stay alive. While we hold the thoughts and dwell on the memories, the feelings are inside our bodies in the form of vibrations and these affect us. While the memory holds the event, situation, or incident, we keep it alive within our cells. It is easy to say, *"forget it"* but not so easy to do.

Did you realise that you can reprogram your memory to do just that. You can actually reprogram your memory on some level to forget the initial incident or experience that cause the problem and massive emotional crisis. Once forgotten it can no longer hurt you.

Anything is possible to overcome once you are ready to let go of the hurt and erase it from your memory. Whatever it is or was can no longer harm us if it no longer exists. This is because once out of the memory, it is as though it no longer exists or has ever existed.

When we reprogram our memory we are only fooling it. On another level, is the thread of knowing that we have actually reprogrammed. We lie to ourselves and live the lie because it is more bearable than the truth. We do really know that we are pretending. It's like a child who wants to be superman and pretends he can fly. Not many actually jump off buildings because they are consciously aware of the fact that it is all make-believe. When circumstances exist where memory contains terror or huge trauma, this is a valid reason. It is like stepping around the problem. Working with vibrational oils and massage can also circumvent or release the emotions locked within the cells of traumatic circumstances and events. Once the emotions are released, the memory released to the past, though still available in the memory banks it is no longer charged with emotion and no longer hurts. Let me explain Lisa's case.

Lisa has experienced date rape, and knows the emotional crippling disease it is. Through reprogramming she is now cured of the negative effects and has gone on to live a normal life without the haunting memories. When people talk of rape, she can actually join in the conversation whereas she used to freeze up and silently relive her nightmare. The feelings and emotions that used to swamp her are gone. Lisa can explain and communicate her experience without breaking down in tears. She has a life again whereas before she reprogrammed her mind she was in an invisible, inner prison.

Please note that this is not a deliberate lie to avoid responsibility, or a denial to save having to make amends, but a method of coping.

Recipe: Reprogramming your Bio-Computer

- Imagine your mind as a giant video-screen.
- Take the unwanted scene and replay it on this screen in black-and-white.
- Shrink the picture and place it in the bottom left corner of the giant screen of your entire mind. It is in the past and unimportant.
- Visualise what you wish had happened. Make the new replacement in colour. Let it fill the whole screen and add emotions and vivid action.
- Having played the scene in your mind, replay it quickly.
- Replay it a third time and then remember remembering.
- Tell your memory you want to remember that experience. If you accidentally go to the small black-and-white picture, pull out and deliberately remember the colour replacement.

You now have a new memory. You WILL know that the replacement is a fake. If asked in a court of law, you will be able to pull details from the correct situation that really did happen, only your emotions will be fooled.

When Lisa finds someone talking about rape, she can now join in the conversation at whatever level she chooses. She is free to tell others what happened to her or to discuss what she has read as though her rape never occurred. She has reprogrammed her mind to give her freedom from nightmares that were haunting her from time to time.

Her success has also helped a client whom I counselled some months later. The young man would not say what the 'terrible deed he committed' was, but the remorse was tearing him apart. He became almost obsessed with wanting to do the impossible—undo the past and make amends but he would not contact anyone to do this. He could not even go home to see his family. His other concern was a girl, whom he hoped would one-day recover, from the terrible thing he did. This young man needed to know that people do eventually cope.

WARNING

Be careful and selective about what you use to replace your unwanted incident, situation, or event! The replacement must be positive and not hurt or injure someone else otherwise it is not releasing and reprogramming the memory but plotting revenge. Revenge is different negative highly charged emotion. Revenge may be a higher emotion than desperation or depression and come through as you progress in clearing the memory but it should not be the focus. No matter how much you may think, they deserve it. Universal law cannot be violated no matter how good you know your reason is. Replay the situation through the eyes of the highest emotion you can at any time until finally you can replay through the eyes of love and all will be well. It is a gradual process.

Let me explain with Lisa's story again:

Recipe: Lisa's Reprogramming

Lisa had believed in the fairy-tail idea of her falling in love with a wonderful guy and all life being wonderful after that. Her only error was that she was a little impatient waiting to get there. Circumstances unfolded that she was raped when she lost her virginity. For her it was total devastation. Whenever she recalled the incident afterwards, she felt stupid for believing the story that led to her being trapped. She felt unclean for being touched and a myriad of other negative emotions all linked to her experience. I am sure many women (and some men) can relate.

Lisa consciously ran through the situation again in her mind with the express purpose of telling her mind how she would have liked to experience that part of her life. She replaced it with herself being wooed and caressed by a person who truly loved her. This replacement took her gently, carefully, and lovingly from one step to another until she and her imagined lover, finally lay spent, at peace, and fulfilled in each other's arms. She replaced her first sexual contact with love, peace, and joy. Gone were the hurt and the emotional violence. The shock of the rape disappeared. She did not replace it with doing her rapist harm, with fighting, or killing him. Just with what she wanted. Lisa needed a memory of love. She used a positive image, which did not harm anyone else, to replace the horror.

Adapting this principle to a particular case will take some time and consideration. It is not a quick and easy thing to do. Although it can be completed in one session, may not be able to be addressed for some time afterwards. While emotions are too raw the memory is too painful and the task seems too difficult.

Prayer

Prayer is a wonderful method of healing that has been used by millions of people. This book would not be complete without mentioning this. I do not intend to argue religion or convince atheists and agnostics that a God exists but prayer is accessible to all—even those who don't believe in a God. Each individual has a right to his or her personal belief and prayer can be viewed in the light as not leaving one stone unturned in the search for wellness or a cure. If healing is available through prayer and we choose not to take advantage of that, OK. BUT what if the answer to your problem lay under that stone you chose not to turn? What if prayer was your answer and you dismissed it and had to keep suffering until . . . ?

If we believe in a Divine Force, no matter what name we give it, we can call on that force for help. Prayer has helped people endure the impossible and survive. Calling on God's help in times of need opens the door to miracles. In some cases of illness and disease, miracles are all that is left. Hope and miracles! At this point many people have found their spirituality.

Often in life we may not get involved in questions of religion, spirituality and what lies beyond death because we are too busy living life. When we get older or become very sick that changes. I have talked to people who felt hypocritical if they only turn to their religion in those times of need. And I noticed others criticise those who found their God in the last few days or hours of their lives. But, why not? What better time is there? Children turn to parents when they have a need and so people turn to their Divine Parent. As the relationship is generally based on love, why not turn in that direction for help? If someone I love needs help, I give it. So does everyone. It is human nature to help in times of need. This is especially evident during natural disasters. Then the best in human nature emerges as whole communities open up to the needs of the needy.

Many church communities have prayer lists for the sick. I have seen miracles happen through these healing lists. Inoperable brain tumours have shrunk to nothing with only the power of prayer. Other terminal patients who were in a state of panic because they have no apparent future, suddenly and peacefully accepted their situation. These people have said good-byes and passed peacefully and serenely from this world to the next. Prayer does not always fulfil our desire exactly as we ask, but it fulfils our need in the best way possible. Sometimes we cannot understand the wisdom in this.

Isn't it strange how often quite naturally say the words, Oh my God—OMG—when something dramatic happens?

The Diversity of Prayer

Prayer is not always performed on bended knee with hands held together. Prayer is talking with God, the Divine Force which is ever present, everywhere, all the time. It is there in your hospital bed. It is in your room in the small hours of the morning. The Force is present in the park. Available to you on the street, it is everywhere. Prayer is connection—communication. It takes place aloud or with the small inner voice, silently. It can also take place through feelings: both voice and feelings are vibrations. And we do not need to sit or kneel still. We can dance our prayer, pray while walking, or just sit in a quiet corner. The important aspect is YOU and YOUR GOD.

When my father had his massive heart attack and lay in hospital in those first vital hours, our friends came forward and began an informal prayer circle. We had many faiths and varieties of prayers. Each person sent out their prayer in their own way and their own time but the common link holding the circle together was my father's welfare. There were Catholics, Lutherans, Anglicans, and non-denominational. The Buddhist meditated as he prayed for him. Father was on Christian Spiritualist healing lists requesting that help go to wherever it is needed for him and his family. One friend prayed to Allah and another in his Jewish way. The Shaman danced her request in to the Great Spirit asking that the healing take place if my father truly desires it. All different religions with the one common link: Prayer to their Divine Force.

Just as there are many ways to pray, there are many types of prayer. We can pray for ourselves and for others. Because we are not all knowing, it is best to pray for the 'best' outcome for whoever is involved. We can pray for strength. We can pray for love and peace. We can even pray for faith.

- Prayer in thanks for the healing that has yet to come is particularly powerful. This is because it assumes the faith that the request has already been fulfilled. It is like the affirmation. It accepts the answer. Prayer for thanks can be made before the condition has taken place in the physical, or afterwards. The emotions of thanks will give extra power to the words and the healing.
- The prayer of request is the most common. It is also the most important. How can we receive if we do not ask?
- The prayer of praise shows us the extent of the power available to help our healing. We should also praise our marvellous body, the health we have, our life, the people we share it with, and so the list becomes endless. When one part does not work we can still praise the miracle of the rest and as such, we are praising

the Divine Creator of All Life. We can sing praise for the healing we have yet to receive, making it an act of faith until it manifests in the physical.

Recipe: Prayer

- Find a quiet place away from distractions. (Even within your mind on a bus is possible)
- Breath out very slowly to relax your body and encourage the alpha mind state
- Speak from the heart
- Leave the situation or problem with the Source

Faith

Faith is the belief in a positive outcome despite current circumstances or facts. An inner knowing that everything will be OK even though it may look totally opposite. This is particularly important in the areas of health. Anyone who is ill might find it particularly difficult to believe in a positive outcome when focusing on the current pain and misery they are feeling. Faith is looking at the desired outcome, believing it is going to happen anyway.

Faith falls into 4 major categories

- faith in self
- faith in health professionals
- faith in the particular set of procedures, modality or processes (the cure) and
- faith in God, Universe or Divine Healing Force.

Faith in yourself as a healer

Healers must have faith in themselves. If you are trying to rid yourself of a bodily condition that you are not happy with, having faith in a desired outcome is important. Doubting will undo the work and a series of doubts alternated with faith will be like going around in circles. If you want to walk across the room and dance two steps forward three back four forward some sideways, you will never progress to your goal. Have faith. Move forward.

Healers know miracles occur and generally have faith in their ability to channel the healing energies and in their openness to let the answer come through. If you are healing yourself, perhaps that self-confidence is missing in your first attempt or even your first few attempts. The more you come to realise that you are unique and a marvellous creation the better it gets. Success should not be confused with a particular outcome because sometimes healing manifest other than we, the healer visualise. In our view the progression is from survival, getting well, and finally to vibrant health. Sometimes that is not the ultimate intention. Sometimes illness is a vehicle to move on. Keeping faith in yourself after experiencing a letting go incident is no more than a test in your confidence.

Know and have faith that what you are doing as a healer for your own health is the right thing, is good, and that it will help you to heal. As you fight the disease, you are returning your body, mind, and spirit to the ease, which is the natural state of health. The more confidence you have in yourself, the better healer you become. There is an upper limit to confidence. Over confidence does lose credibility with others and with your inner self.

Recipe: Faith in self

- Take a moment to quieten your mind
- Breath out very slowly to relax your body and encourage the alpha mind state
- Speak to your inner self—your heart
- Feel your connection to the universe and
- Know in your source that you are powerful.

Faith in your medical practitioner

We should have faith in our medical practitioner or health professional. He or she is the trained expert with experience and knowledge. Faith in the abilities of your practitioner leads to faith in recommendations and belief in the guidance and advice they give. In my view the first step of any healing is finding the correct diagnosis. Once we can know what we are fighting the mind will often open to the possibilities. Occasionally with a major health challenge the mind will close and give up because it views the challenge insurmountable. Without a diagnosis, we are often lost in a sea of searching. While our goal is unclear the outcome seems unachievable. Once the diagnosis is established a prognosis can be developed and we can choose the right path for a cure. Without it, we are often lost because we are creatures of habit and like to see a physical path. This is not always the case. Miracles and vibrational healing can go straight to the solution without the time space containing all the steps between. Miracles take a lot of faith.

Faith in your "cure"

Faith in a cure is a belief that whatever procedures we follow will work.

Placebos work because of the faith in their power. When my children were small one of them got warts. Instead of going to a chemist and getting an ointment I gave them a small bottle of water and told them to brush it on carefully morning and night but to be careful not to spill it on any other part of their body. The warts disappeared in no time. Healed with their belief in the miracle in the bottle! They did wake up to what was in the bottle a few years later.

Continually affirming thoughts of a positive outcome builds faith. Focus on the percentage of people your cure has worked on before. Focus on the positive outcome. If you are doing a number of things to help yourself, realise that each has some power, and that the combination of all has added strength. As many hands make light work, many aspects of healing used in combination will often be more powerful. Take the medicine the doctor gives you. Check with the doctor before adding any supplements in case they work against each other. Believe your medication will work. Visualise the process working and giving you the desired outcome. Concentrate on that goal by pretending it has happened. Live it now. Adding power through affirming your health and seeing yourself well will speed up any healing process. Each healing technique you use will add just that little bit more energy to your recovery and eventual wellness.

Be careful because this also works in the negative. Believe that it won't work and you will struggle in your battle back to good health.

Faith in a Supreme Being

Having faith in the Supreme Being is the spiritual sanctuary from possible negative outcomes. Having faith in Divine Healing links you to ultimate power. It is sometimes the hardest faith to have because it comes with some difficult questions. Sometimes it comes with doubts. How can the Divine Force be good if our child, spouse, lover, or we ourselves catch diseases, suffer pain or worse still—die? Is it really our God punishing us? Perhaps we have drawn the condition to us? How and why would we do such a thing? This entanglement of personal belief is based on parental and religious teaching plus a heap of thoughts and ideas presented to us throughout our entire lives.

I know that faith in our Divine Force will aid healing immeasurably. When I call on God to help me send healing to someone, I can feel the energy surge flow through me.

Sometimes life wears me thin and I get stressed. At those times it is sometimes hard to focus thoughts on good outcomes. Watching TV news or current affairs sometimes leads to entrapment in terror, fear of the future, worries that humanity is deteriorating and having faith in the positive gets difficult. Then I naturally get disconnected with my faith.

Death is part of life but when we are close to someone special, their death or merely the possibility of their death becomes impossible to fathom. Intellectually we know that death is inevitable but emotionally we feel we cannot live without them. Surely a loving God would not allow their passing to happen. We lose faith although life is actually eternal. It is only the body that is limited. I know I was spirit before I was in this body, I am spirit now and I will be spirit after I leave my body. Death is no reason to lose faith. It is just that we are so conditioned by this physical life and sometimes forget that we are more.

Rebuilding faith

When I lack faith in my path or my connection to God, the Devine Source, I go out in nature and look at the trees and flowers. Huge trees stand for decades having grown from the tiniest of seeds. When I see them I remember the awesomeness of life. As I admire nature, I reconnect with the Force. I then feel ashamed and wonder why I ever doubted in the first place. I know it is the decrease in personal energy that makes me vulnerable to negatives. Sometimes it is just what life dished out. Challenges occur and give us the ingredients to make life interesting. Decisions and choices I make affect my energy levels and my ability to withstand these challenges. Everything from the food I eat to the thoughts I have affect me on some level. These choices are my power to create my life, my state of health, even my levels of belief in the Divine healing force.

It is from nature that I have learnt to look at the bigger picture. The final outcome of any situation is not always clear at every moment in time. All the separate incidents that happen to me are somehow parts of the same Divine Plan.

Recipes for building Faith in God

- Set your mind with the intention of calling on God for help
- Breath out very slowly to relax your body and encourage your connection then draw on the power Breath out very slowly to relax your body and encourage your connection then draw on the power
- Remember how you grew inside your mother from two cells and were born as a baby
- Lose yourself in something you love—dancing, fishing, painting . . . . Feel the universal energy of perfection
- Pray
- Read about miracles
- Spend time in awe of all the wonderful things that have happened in your life, in the lives of your family & friends
- Realise that you are a child of the God—a part of the Universe—one with all that is—loved, protected and deserving of all the good there is
- Walk in nature admiring the miracles of life. Watching a nature film will do too.)

Learning to Die

Please note—if this chapter does not agree with your religious views you may choose to simply disregard it. The rest of the book may still have many beneficial ideas that you can adapt. Perhaps the ideas here are something you may choose to ponder someday but cannot adapt at the moment. Religious views of the hereafter are both personal and sacred and I respect every person's right to his or her own beliefs.

We all eventually die. We are born and we die. In understanding the inevitable, we can learn to cope with it. Often it is only a fear of dying and not death itself that we cannot cope with. Anyone not afraid of death is free to really live. My father had a massive heart-attack and died. The doctors worked furiously and he returned to life. From that moment on he never feared death again. While he had many further visits to hospitals over the years and wanted to continue living, he was not afraid to die.

THE WHEEL OF LIFE

Sleep has been called the little death. In a sense, this is true. Our life is broken up into conscious waking periods and unconscious sleep periods. In these sleep times we travel off into a land of dreams. We can go deep within our past or travel to wondrous places. We can talk to relatives long dead and do impossible tasks. We have good dreams and return happy, and we go to places of confusion, which we call nightmares. There is so much out there we do not understand. Life here on this planet is divided into these periods of awake in the conscious mind and asleep in the dream type state or in the unconscious.

Every day we live through the day and dream through the little death of sleep at night.

What if our whole life is but an extension of this? What if our life is the big conscious state? Then death could be described as the dream of the big sleep. What if life and death then were nothing more than a larger cycle of the conscious and unconscious: of the waking and dream/sleep of each day and night? Would it then be so unnatural or fearful to die?

We sleep because we are tired and need to rejuvenate. We die because our body is tired and we need the big sleep. Whatever we believe of the hereafter and death, we need to see the peace and beauty rather than face it with fear. As we learn about how to die and are prepared in our own way, death is no longer a monster to be feared but an inevitable experience we will conquer. Without fear of death, we can also truly live, knowing both life and death are separate processes we go through. When you put the fear and doubt of dying behind you, you feel prepared for whenever may come. It is like making a decision. While you do not know what to do, you are lost but once you decide, then the road is clear. Once prepared, the agony and fear of the unknown is conquered. This act delivers freedom. Freedom is perfectly in tune with the healing vibration.

One reader of my first edition was given my book and after reading this chapter was resting at home and facing palliative care. She lost her fear of dying, continued to enjoy life and finally passed on more than a decade later.

How to Die

Death comes in two ways and I have been told it is our choice which one we take—either fast or slow. In cases if illness and disease dying will happen slowly, whereas walking in front of a fast moving object will make it happen almost instantaneously. Either is a means to an end. If the body is going to have major physical harm, we often leave beforehand. Many stories of people who have had near death experiences have confirmed this. The car has crashed and they have seen it from some distance away, finally coming to realise that they were the individual in the car and then waking up in hospital.

When the dying process begins, it is beneficial to focus on the journey ahead. This is where religion and belief are important. It sets the goal or at least the name of the goal we are heading for. We go where we expect to go. It matters not whether we call it Heaven beyond or we look to Mecca, or fly to the Happy Hunting Ground. We go wherever is right for us personally. There is a special place for us all.

Even if we have no religion or have never been to any type of church in our lives, we can go towards the Light and the Source. At this time life becomes a fog. The fog is the transition between the level of existence we enjoy physically on earth and the next. Some people have described it like being in a bubble that separates the event from all else. We may see loved ones who have passed over before. They come into this place in time and space. While we are in this transition between the two worlds, those people who are with us may hear us talking and think we are delirious or babbling nonsense. This is because they may not see what we are aware of, or understand what is happening. Their words are muffled and sound like they are a long way away.

There is a time for letting go of the emotions, people, places, and situations that keep us in this life. There is a time for seeking and getting forgiveness. And there is the looking forwards and moving towards the Light.

Dying is a process of dissolving this life and an emergence into another state of being. If you believe there is life and then nothing. That is what you will probably find yourself in. You will experience the nothingness which is completely consistent with your beliefs. Perhaps after experiencing nothingness for a while you may awaken to a thought and question "Is this all there is?" at which point you may start seeing something more.

One individual I know finds peace and solitude by meditating in a place of nothingness. He describes it as an absence of sound and light, people and things. Nothingness is a place of perfection for him. A place in where he feels safe. He returns from there rejuvenated, happy, and at peace. It is his special place. Everyone finds his or her own special place. Mine is in nature around a fire with my family.

Some find a tunnel, some a staircase and others float up a path. Whatever feels right is right. It matters which road we take, they all lead to the same place.

We all come into this world through a physical path, which we share only with siblings, yet we all are born the same way. We are born into this life on this planet. And so the leaving is the same. Each of us leaves his or her body in their individual way, and returns to the beyond. We go back to the Source.

Dying is a process of mind and spirit as much as a letting go of physical body. At the end of life we let go of the body just as at the end of the day we discard our clothes. As long as you concentrate on Love and Light, you will be safe in your journey.

I believe that eventually we all get there despite what we may believe on the way through. Negatives only mean the road is longer and harder.

Why suffer unnecessarily when it serves no purpose. You wouldn't take off your pants by squeezing your body through one of the pants legs. We are Source energy and return to Source. Love and light is the direct route.

Recipe: Practice Dying

There are four simple steps, which we can practice in our mind, so that when our time comes, we can just follow without thinking. It is visualisation of the dying process so that when we face it we have no fear. Running through this visualisation a few times does not draw it in for that is not the intention. The intention is simply to lay a road for whenever the time comes. By no means dwell on this recipe.

- See the Light. It comes from your Divine Force.
- Surround yourself with the Light and let the Light penetrate your whole being. Ask yourself and the Light for forgiveness for the unfinished, the words and incidents you regret, that you can let go and drop those burdens. Receive the ultimate forgiveness from the Divine Source, for only goodness can melt away all negatives.
- Become one with the Light. This is a two-way action. The Light becomes part of you and you become part of the Light. Then you are one.
- Move with the Light back to the Source.

The dying process is as individual as our religious beliefs. Instead of the Light, you may picture the form of a powerful angel, or a special Being. Or you may just walk with loved ones into a lovely garden.

Whether you say "God's Children return to Him", refer to passing as being one with Buddha or Allah, or think of joining the elders in the Happy Hunting Ground, the message and meaning is the same. Final destination—being home, happy and at peace—whatever that is for you.

Learning to Live

Life is precious but people are so wrapped in their busy world, they do not realise this fact. One of the benefits of illness is that we are reminded of riches we have in this life that often go unnoticed. Some of the little gifts in your life that may be hovering for you to notice

- Sunshine and natural surroundings
- flowers in gardens and parks
- children playing, dogs barking and people having fun
- special people in your life
- your job giving you the ability to meet financial obligations
- the house you live in that keeps out the weather
- shops giving you options of millions of items at your fingertips
- whatever . . . . (Use your imagination.)

Many of us are like John. Perhaps you can relate to his story?

John spent his life striving to be the best. He had a brilliant career, a family, and a beautiful house with little time to enjoy it. He also had a report from his doctor that showed he had a particular cancer which was so advanced there was no expected cure. He had 6 weeks to live.

He went home on the night he was given the 'death prediction' and as he walked towards his house he had a surreal experience. He was interrupted during his mental raving while telling God he was given an unfair deal. John began to see his garden in a new light. He saw the sun set and recognised the awesome beauty. New emotions flooded into him.

Finally, he wiped the tears from his face. He began to see what he had not seen in many years. He saw the love he shared with his wife and children. He saw his business for the current cash-flow it really was. He realised his life was not his position, his work, or his body. His life was the precious spark of energy that kept it all going.

We don't have to be under a sentence of potential death to recognise the beauty in life. Yes, in our hectic life we forget about the preciousness of life. Only when we think of it being taken away do we see our real life and what is important to us. How much would your goals change if you knew you had only a week to live?

Anna, had been fighting cancer for years and suddenly her blood cancer-count began rising. The doctors gave her an operation and explained she would only have a matter of weeks. It was sad but she had the chance to say good-bye to her family and friends. She made peace with people, herself, and God. Finally she floated off at peace. Anna died slowly.

What of the person suddenly killed in an accident? They have no time to say:—"Stop I need to tell my children I love them; I want to hug my lover one more time; I want to apologise; To make amends; To prepare." They don't have the time to say a leisurely good-bye or to just watch that one last movie they want to see or anything . . .

What we probably all need to do is to really live while we can. Without dwelling on death, we need to truly live our life to the full and fill it with the experiences and people we cherish. We need to hug our loved ones before they leave in the morning, take the time to tell someone we love them, help someone in need, do, be and enjoy what really makes us happy—without being totally selfish about it. We need to enjoy the time we have here expecting a great future but knowing we have only this one-day at a time.

It is sad that we often do not realise how precious life is until we are threatened with its loss. In fact, life is just as precious five minutes before we are given six months to live, as it is five minutes after. We just understand the concept of preciousness much better in the second instance.

Recipe: Live Today

- Cut time into this day today and the future
- Forget the promise and illusion of tomorrow
- Make today count

You can still defer jobs into the future, make plans for a life-time but the focus is on today.

- Start today and live each day like it was the last.

Time is an invention related to the number of revolutions the earth makes around the sun. It is abstract and quite meaningless when you consider that you only live in one moment. This moment of now! We all have only one day at a time made up of moment by moment. The doctor giving the time limit and the patient receiving it, both have only this moment of now. The new-born babe and the hundred-year-old man, both live only this moment of now. Just like you and me. Everyone only lives in now. As long as your now is good, that is all that matters. If now isn't good, use the time productively—project ahead and create a better tomorrow all the time feeling the good that will come. What you feel is in the present "now" time-space even if you are thinking of the past or the future.

Life can be put in a different perspective. Living life consciously by focusing on the moments will bring out the preciousness. The small annoying things like spilled coffee suddenly lose their impact. The future is important to plan for and bills have to be paid but focus is on enjoyment rather than fears of things that may or may not happen. It does not translate into being selfish and irresponsible such as spending an entire month's wages on a new dress or pair of shoes to make you feel good. Nor does it translate into total indulgence and deciding to spend the day in bed rather than showing up for another day's work.

How many of us truly know they will be here tomorrow? We assume we will and we prepare as though we will. The important things should be done TODAY.

Here is a list of *"things to do today"* I like to focus on

- Holding a loved one.
- Calling my mother.
- Staying in touch with friends.
- Forgiving myself for the dumb things I sometimes do.
- Enjoying a drink and a meal.
- Taking the chance!
- Being happy.
- Making others laugh.

Sometimes I have others on my list too but being happy is quite consistently there. It is no mystery that the secret to a happy life is to have a long string of happy days, each following the other. So how do you have a happy day> you might ask. Think happy thoughts. Take part in activities you enjoy and take each day with ease. Don't sweat the small stuff understanding that everything is small stuff if you take the longer view. Take care to live quality and let the small annoyances disappear without notice. By focusing your thoughts and feelings on happiness you will be vibrating happiness out into the universe and by the universal Law of Attraction it will be drawn back to you. Whilst this formula will not guarantee your future will not contain anything that you would consider bad or unpleasant, it will puts the odds in your favour and give you a much better experience of tolerating the present. In any case it can do no harm to live and enjoy each day as it comes. Some are good days and some are better days yet all are wonderful because we are alive to live them.

Living in the moment

When my parents were growing up there were few telephones and TV had not invented. Evenings were spent with the family and they would listen to the news and special programs occasionally on the radio. When I grew up every house had a telephone, we got mail delivered daily and people started watching TV every evening.

With the invention of mobile phones came the idea that we are important and busy and our lifestyle became hectic. Life also lost a lot of it's quality. Lots of families don't sit down to dinners together, people can't spell or ever write letters and conversations about "real-life" TV hit the internet. People even interrupt phone conversations with phone conversations. People don't have time anymore. They are stressed and depressed. Some reach out on an emotional level filling that gap with food becoming obese to compensate what they perceive they have missed out on. Many do not know that with the high use of technology their energy is being robbed. They are really reaching out for simple human contact that would give them spiritual connection and enhanced their energy flows. Test the concept for yourself. Spend an hour behind a computer and get in touch with your energy levels and you will notice that they will have gone down. If you spent the time escaping into a game you may fell excited and high but your energy levels will have still gone down. You need a coke or V. Spend an hour with great friends over a cup of coffee and unless the conversation was completely negative, you will feel good and happy.

Recipe: To Indulge in the moment

Do this exercise alone, in nature or with a friend

- Turn off the mobile or put it on silent and away
- Just enjoy and experience the quality of the moment
- When your mind tells you "this is boring" smile
- Listen to the sounds of life around you
- If you feel like painting, paint
- If you feel like writing, write.

Whatever you are doing, do only that without interruption.

I have lunch at the office and the girls sometimes do not understand why I don't always choose to join them and like to sit quietly at my desk instead. At my desk I can do things uninterrupted. If I go on a website I can read and search without distraction. When I sit with the girls for lunch I enjoy the interaction and conversation but few can come without their mobiles. In the middle of discussions they will get a funny email or text that they just have to share with the one sitting beside them or have to read right now. Not once have the interruptions been a sick child they had to attend to or something really important. It seems that everything outside is more important than actually listening what is being said. I know that is the habit and current character of young people and they are not doing any harm but their behaviour detracts from the quality of the moment. I am not expecting that people don't get bored with other people's thoughts and ideas but giving people the courtesy of your undivided attention is disappearing and that detracts from the situation and quality of the connection.

Relationships of all kinds suffer from communication interruptis. Can you imagine being with the one you love, you want to tell them how much they mean to you and the mobile rings, they talk to someone else and have a laugh and a joke, set up a meeting and discuss how a third person felt about some incident that has nothing to do with you.

It really kills the moment! I realise that some people are tied to phones for their jobs and totally understand having to be kept informed. The police commissioner will need to know if an officer has been shot as soon as it happens but when we catch up for a short lunch with a friend we need to enjoy that experience totally and without interruption. If you focus on every moment and keep it as clear and isolated as possible, life takes on a whole new level of quality. Families who go camping together, bush walkers and simple pleasures like playing board games enhance human interaction and build connections.

Joking and laughter are a wonderful way of building energy and enjoying the moment. I am very lucky to be currently working with a wonderful group of people who are led by a man who has old fashioned values. He likes to be a comedian and encourages friendly nicknames and having a laugh. He has seen friends killed during their workday and been impacted by the effect of that on their friends, family and loved ones. He also shares my view that you are at work for a substantial part of the day and if you can make the work-place enjoyable then work can be fun. The positive effect that has on quality of work is amazing.

Facebook is a tool—a wonderful way of communicating and making people feel important. It has also led to suicides through cyber bullying. Emails are similar. An email gets the message through, is really convenient in conveying facts and wonderful for sending everything from pictures to loving thoughts but still restricts the quality of connection. Conversations give instant feedback because through conversations you pick up more than just the words. You pick up feelings. In emails you can influence people without having to face them but you miss the way it is said, the tones of the words that give you a clue how sincere the message really is. I can lie on paper much more easily that I can lie to someone sitting opposite me. They will see my facial expression, the direction of my eyes—my body language and that adds more than half of the connection we get from others. Emotion carries in the vibration of our voice. Seeing a tear behind the eye of someone can melt your heart. All those communication clues are missing from a Facebook or email message. The bulk of our communication is more than data or information. It is the spirit to spirit vibrational connection brings in quality. And interrupting that interaction with an incoming mobile call just detracts so enormously from experiencing and indulging in the moment. Holidays are so wonderful because of that lack of interruption.

People who are sick particularly need quality and enhanced vibrations of fun and love. They need to know they are important to you and they need the human touch and interaction. Give lots of hugs and visits and be the healer that is lurking within you. It is very, very rewarding!

If you are sick, let friends help you. Accept the love behind the visits. Enjoy the interaction of conversations and let the quality of each moment be the best it can be. If you are alone, imagine the love flowing to you. Make up a lover if you have to. Your mind will not know the difference and as long as your body feels the improvement, healing is lurking! It all in the vibe!

PART THREE

The Ultimate Recipe

When Jesus Christ walked the earth he made an enormous impact on people. His teachings are still being followed today although the message is sometimes a little blurred from his original. He is referred to as the light of the world due to the knowledge he imparted on humanity. It is this knowledge on how to live a good life, how to treat fellow humans and how to remain healthy and on our chosen spiritual path by following our energy that is just as relevant today as it was 2000 years ago. It was only explained a bit different due to the politics and simple minds of the people he was teaching at the time. Christ taught mankind to focus on personal vibrations and the fact that we are spirit in a physical body and experiencing life filtered through our minds. He taught us to separate what is spiritual guidance and manmade laws that need to be followed in order for society to work. We may be free spirits but when we are driving on a road we need to obey the speed limit signs and the red light when it shines, we have to stay on our side of the road or we experience the consequences. For sinning—doing the wrong thing—we are punished by God—the Universe. We reap the rewards of negative behaviour as we get a traffic fine which causes grief to our wallet and can stop that freedom by forfeiting our permission to drive—we may lose our driver's licence or we might experience much more serious consequences through a collision that may cause loss of life. All the concepts and guidance depend on the choice of words used in communication. The message is the same. Remain positive, do the right thing, love and look after yourself and others and your life will be good. Life is just a series of choices that result in outcomes, events and experiences. Looking below this level is the energy that is the currency of life. Doing something with evil intent is sending out negative energy and by the law of attraction what is sent out returns magnified. Yet there is no law that says that bad things cannot happen to good people. All is simply experience and circumstances that affect us and others in the school that is our lifelong learning journey.

The basis of the ultimate recipe is the fact that fundamentally each of us is energy. We are made up of skin and bones, organs and blood. On a much smaller quantum physics level we are cells and elements and atoms. Atoms are mostly empty space—a nucleus with electrons whizzing around them. It is that which makes us energy. The electrons are whizzing so fast that they seem solid.

Everything is made this way and has a measureable electromagnetic frequency. Furniture has it, animals have it, plants and rocks have it. Humans have it. The difference between the electromagnetic frequency or level of vibration between something alive and something inanimate such as a chair is that things that are alive also have a capacity of mind. This mind will enable birds to tune in through instinct and know where to fly for winter or how to construct a nest without planned drawings and instructions when they may have never made one before. For humans it even goes further as we have the ability to think and make choices. We can choose what we do or say. We can project ahead to a desired outcome and chose to follow the steps to reach it. We can choose harmony or imbalance. The natural state for humans is abundant, vibrant health but with the power of choice and focus of desires, outcomes do not always create balance and harmony in the body. Returning to that state of balance is healing and it can occur instantaneously, which we call a miracle or over a period of time. Time is only the earth-bound concept man sticks to counting the revolutions of the planet we live on. In relation to health and well-being time is a mere technicality. It is vibration levels or frequency that is important.

Vibrational Healing

In terms of measurable electromagnetic frequency a healthy human body has 62-68 MHz (Megahertz). If this frequency drops through stress, undernourishment or a myriad of possible reasons imbalance occurs. Imbalance will let disease and problems exist in the body. Cold and flu symptoms can happily thrive in a body that has dropped to 58 MHz while viruses love a few megs below that. Chronic fatigue patients register 52 MHz as does the Epstein Barr virus. Cancer can only thrive around 42 MHz. Interestingly enough chemotherapy drops the body below that frequency and the cancer can no longer exist. The process of dying begins once frequency drops below 25 MHz and is held there for a period of time.

I once had a client who had learnt this information and decided she wanted to use it to commit suicide. She did not initially convey this to me because she was an attendee at a workshop on vibrational oils I was teaching at the time. During the course of the day we worked with an oil blend called Hope. It contains a mixture of pure essential oils that uplift the spirit by raising vibrations. She was particularly drawn to the oil which is a sign that she really needed the energy on some level—physical, spiritual or emotional. I know it was not her time to go and the suicidal thoughts were a result of the chronic fatigue she had been suffering for over a decade at that time. She lavished the oil on her skin, breathed the oil deep into her lungs and started smiling. The joy that shone on her face was lovely to see. I knew she was healing on an emotional level beyond her own temporary ideas. When she recognised the change in her frequency and happy mood she confessed her ultimate reason for attending the seminar and was angry that I had interfered in her plans. I did not impose my ideas on her. My workshop merely educated the participants on what they can do to enhance their vibration to improve health and happiness. Anyone who was drawn to particular oil was given permission to use as much as they required of it. No-one was forced to participate or sample the oils. She also told me how disappointed she was at the lack of outcome of the afternoon. "It was a waste of time really". I have a totally different view. I had a participant who was contemplating suicide to the degree that she had marked the day in her diary and sorted a to do list giving all her possessions away. She even planned to get her pet dogs put to sleep the day before. After the work-shop she got her house in order, and started travelling taking her animals with her. She returned to embrace and enjoy life. I believe the oils took her out of her momentary wrong thought-patters by raising her vibrations and bringing her electromagnetic body into balance so she could begin making better choices. She experienced a vibrational healing and the results manifested quickly. Anyone can do that given the right recipes and the right tools.

Recipe—In God's hands

- Breath out 3 times, each time going deeper into relaxation
- In your mind's eye see yourself as energy
- Notice that everything around you is energy too
- Reach high into the universe and notice the energy.
- You are one with the universal source energy.
- It flows through you. It is you and you are it.
- Hold yourself within the energy for 5 to 25 minutes—in God's Hands.

Note: You cannot overdo this exercise. My father did this type of exercise many times through the day after he had suffered a massive heart-attack while waiting for by-pass surgery. When doctors finally opened his chest they found he did not need a triple by-pass because his heart had healed itself somewhat and a double bypass was all he needed.

Tools for enhancing your vibration

The object of vibrational healing is to raise the electromagnetic frequency or vibration to a healthy level and maintain it for the long term. In the text above I mentioned vibrational or pure essential oils. It has been scientifically proven that using oils can increase the body's frequency by 10 MHz.

Music is sound and sound is vibration. Music that is balanced like that of the great masters is very beneficial and can raise vibrations. Have you noticed that opera, church hymns and marching music makes you feel different. The lively tunes from Ireland make you want to dance. Any music that lifts your spirits will lift your vibration except heavy metal and hard-rock. Extremely loud music can actually cause harm to the subtle energy bodies that surround you.

Walking in nature is very beneficial to raising personal vibrations and spirits. The exercise is good for the muscles and clearing the lymphatic system but looking at nature and being drawn into the activities of such things as listening to birds, being lost in the beauty of a flower or being in awe of the grand scale of some of earth's wonderful landscapes lifts the spirits. It can even clear depression.

Rocks and crystals are known for their vibrational healing potential. Just as a copper bangle can help relieve pain of some arthritis sufferers, various minerals have particular frequencies and can be matched to re-establish balance. Mineralogy is a fascinating subject to study and believing that the stones have the power to heal will make them more effective. With all varieties of vibrational healing, it is the intent behind the tool which is often more important than the tool itself.

Carrying a talisman or lucky charm is working the placebo effect. Whether it is a lucky travel Buddha or a rabbit's foot, charms are only as strong as our belief in them. Of course sometimes even beliefs fail. Once events are set in motion and desired outcomes requested of the Law of Attraction, the delivery will occur time unspecific. You will get what you ask for whether you want it or not. As long as the fear of the outcome is not stronger than the faith in it, this will work. If the fear is the greater then it is the negative that is actually being ordered in the attraction.

Sacred objects such as the family Bible, special object belonging to a loved one or objects given or made with love carry a special vibration. Psychics can often pick up some of the vibrations on personal objects and give readings from them. If something is precious or valued, it can carry a higher vibration. Often people keep items of clothing or loved items of family members who have passed to keep the memory alive. Tuning into the personal vibration of a loved one, passed or otherwise, enhances our connection with them.

Words carry vibrations. Words like gratitude, love and joy carry a high vibration. Japanese studies of the effect of words on water, has shown some fantastic information. Water was placed over words like love and gratitude for a period of time, then frozen and the ice crystals photographed. They were truly magnificent. Negative words like fear and hate produced unbalanced and odd shaped crystals as opposed to the stunning beauty and perfect balance in the structure of the word love.

Recipe—Making holy water

- Take a bottle of water—the purer the better
- Write the words—Love and gratitude on a piece of paper
- Stand the water bottle directly on the words for a full 24 hours.
- The water will absorb the vibration of the words and change.
- Drink as required
- Simply understanding the power of the vibration within the water will raise your vibration

Water that comes directly from rain carries a vibration until it has been stored and sits still for some time. This is why plants grow better after rain than being watered. They receive and absorb the energy which comes down with the rain that is not present in mains water. When a spring gurgles through nature, the water carries a high frequency which is beneficial to health. Polluted water on the other hand is toxic in more than just the chemicals it may carry. The vibrations or frequencies within this water are foul. The most interesting thing is that this foul toxic water can have its vibration enhanced by prayer. The structure of the crystals within the water actually changes. Check out the work of Mr Emoto.

My grandmother would never eat a meal without the ritual of prayer and giving thanks. Although it is not tested yet, perhaps the words affect water molecules within food in the same way and balance not only the body preparing it for digestion, the mind for accepting sustenance but the food itself as well. Quantum physics has so much more that it can tell us and the miracles do not get minimised in the discovery of the knowledge. I recall the moment when I recognised that the sparkles I was seeing in the air all about me was actually the energy in the rain that was falling. Pure magic!

Objects carry the vibration of people who have touched them. Much like fingerprints that can identify someone's touch, vibrations can be left for others to tune into. Psychics call this method of reading psychometry. This is why good card readers cleanse the decks between clients. As someone shuffles the deck of cards while focusing inwards, an impression or vibration is created on the cards. This vibration links the reader to the client once they start reading. The concept is like Hansel and Gretel leaving a trail of food to get back home. Of course the danger for those who are not sensitive enough to pick up the vibration is that they will not recognise the difference between a true psychic and a charlatan. Some people doubt the information because they cannot see or understand the process of how it works yet we all use computers and signals from satellites without really understanding how it all works.

The Negative surge—How you will recognise it is working

Progress in our life's journey is measured in lessons we have learnt. The more we learn the more we become in tune with our path. Musicians practice and get better. Over time artists discover more techniques and paint more interesting artwork. In each profession trade or work, we put in effort and become more than we were before. Increase is the natural order of the universe. In the process we raise our personal vibration.

When I was in my 20s I spent some time studying the Bible and going to church. At that time I noticed that as I worked on building my faith and growing spiritually, negative forces seemed to increase. My priest at the time explained it as the devil drawing you back as soon as you take a step closer to God. As we do our Christian duty and become closer to our maker this battle between the opposing forces gets more intense.

Now I would use different words to explain the process. As an individual raises their vibrational level and sees more clearly, they become aware of negatives that they were previously not aware of. A young child will walk out on a road not seeing the danger while an older child will be aware of the negative consequences associated with that action. Consider domestic violence. While people think it is acceptable the practice will continue. Once realisation that it is wrong occurs then negative behaviour is recognised and a change will occur. Learning makes the difference. Any addict can recognise their problem and begin to understand the fallout once they realise and accept the error of their ways. While we do not think we have power to change or improve ourselves we are victims. Once we recognise anything as a problem, we have raised our vibration. Then it takes courage and work but the solution is within reach. This process transforms victims into success. Look at the problems around you, realise that you are more and better than that, step beyond and your healing has begun. It just may take some time to materialise completely into the physical. While the energies are transforming your life and circumstances, it is beneficial to focus on the desired outcome and practice actions consistent with that. If you want to be a slim and fit person, can see yourself being slim and trim, it is also a good idea to exercise instead of constantly eating sweets. Actions speak louder than words and over time beliefs erode if no positive change is detected.

PART FOUR

PUTTING IT ALL TOGETHER—
You personal recipe

Whether you are facing a terminal illness or want to stop catching every virus that comes your way. If your problem is lack of cash-flow or lack of commitment to a diet, it is simply a problem where current events and circumstances are not consistent with your desires. Whether we want to heal ourselves or others; whether we want to prevent or cure the ill, EVERY TECHNIQUE WORKS towards a solution to some degree. Combining techniques can give us the unique combination correct for each of us individually. This is where the art of healing comes in.

Each of us is capable of choosing what is best for us at any given time. We need only ask ourselves the question and then give possible answers. Deep inside ourselves we will get a feeling. Gut feeling will almost always be right. We can also flip a coin for a positive yes or no, then go with the feeling we get from the result.

Just try it on something simple. Should I go to the library with Mary? Flip. Answer yes. A feeling to either confirm that you want to go, or a feeling of disappointment that you have to go. You carry every true answer within. The coin has been a tool to let you find the true answer. YOU

ARE THE EXPERT. You are the healer who knows what is best for you. Consider the advice from your doctor who has spent years studying. If you do not agree with your chosen expert doctor, get another opinion. This medical opinion should come from another health professional and not from your neighbour. It never ceases to amaze me that people will call a plumber because the roof leaks and have an accountant work out their tax but ask just anybody about health matters. For our health and the sake of our future, we deserve the best.

When faced with a health problem, combining healing techniques is like hitting the problem with a continual bombardment of health. No disease can flourish amongst abundant health, in a clean body and open mind, or simultaneously with great healing vibrations. Health and disease are opposite sides of the same coin. The two are incompatible because they are on contrasting sides of the energy scale.

CAVIAT: If you are on medication and are trying to heal yourself, check with your doctor before taking complimentary medicines in case they clash. Nothing will change if you are taking one substance to pull left and another to pull right.

Build your plan for health by using whatever feels right to you. It may be:

1. Doctor & medication;
2. Meditation for peace of mind;
3. Visualisation of vibrant health;
4. Affirmation that all is well;
5. Prayer for Divine Guidance and Healing;
6. Doing something special every day.

You may be healthy and your list is designed to retain your vibrant health. It may read:

1. Affirmation;
2. Walking and exercise;

3. Meditation to retain balance in all aspects of life;
4. Vibrational oil for creating
5. Eating fresh, healthy food and using supplements;
   and further numbers would be devoted to other areas of life. They could include increasing financial health, job satisfaction, family, and/ or career goals so on.

Goal Setting & evoking the law of attraction

Goals give us the target to shoot for. To set goals begin with a sheet of paper and list what you want to have and achieve. Categorising into four sections will make the process easier to manage.

1. Immediate,
2. this year for short term,
3. the next ten years for long term, and
4. life goals.

And goals can be in any area of our lives. They may include other things beside abundant health or the dream to be perfectly fit. These other goals add incentive for staying healthy or being healed.

- Dream of a new car;
- the house being paid for;
- or dream of taking your special someone to the South Pole for a holiday.
- Whatever your heart desires . . .

This is a part of learning how to really live. Once you have your goals, you can energise them into existence.

If your state of health will not allow you to actually do or physically follow through, this does not matter. The mind is such a strange mechanism, it cannot differentiate between something happening in real life and something just happening in the imagination. Live the dream in the imagination and the body will benefit. Just as you cringe in a movie when something undesirable happens, so you can fool your body into experiencing what you want. When I go to the dentist I lie down on the beach and imagine work-men repairing a wall behind me. I get some weird looks from dentists when they have to tell me a couple of times that it is time to rinse and I don't react immediately, but I take my mind away from that awful drilling. The distraction served Its purpose.

Just a small note of warning: Do not work on more than three to five goals in this way at one time. Too many goals spreads the energy. This means that less energy can be focused on any particular to one. It is far better to work on them in turn, returning for another session later. Spend one to three weeks at a time on each.

Recipe: Energising goals

- Write out each of your goals.
- Start with "I really want . . . .
- Then write at least 10-12 positive statements about how wonderful it is to have . . .

Explain in the positive such things as "I want to feel well because it makes everyone smile. When I am healthy my family is happy. I get joy out of seeing my children laugh.

- Rewrite a set morning and night each day for a week. (Or at least read the ones written earlier to keep the energy consistent and flowing.) Use this exercise in conjunction with or separate from the Gold Card recipe.

The purpose of this recipe is to focus a prolonged time in totally positive thoughts and vibrations of the emotion you want to feel. The Law of Attraction will draw it in and attract more like thoughts and vibrations.

If you do not like writing, simply follow the same procedure in a visualisation. Simply relax and say it to yourself in your head.

Building your personal life-plan can be quite interesting. It begins with your list of goals and moves to planning the path of how you will achieve them. Decide why this is the correct path for you and then do the exercises you set for yourself. Follow through to success by persisting in a devotion to completion.

Keep reading, learning, and modifying according to your growth and development through the ever-present changes that make life interesting and challenging. Enjoy yourself by having lots of fun along the way.

Daily commitment of time to health or any life improvement you have planned is essential. Especially until you have formed a habit of healthful living. Monitor yourself with the help of a diary or weekly chart pinned in a prominent position. On the refrigerator is a good place. The diary reinforces your work by keeping your goals in sight. It keeps the focus clear on the correct path, and makes sure we actually do those techniques we planned. It's like writing your life-story before it happens and then going over and over until it is so familiar it is almost like it has already happened. Without the reminder of a diary or weekly-worksheet, we forget. We forget we have committed ourselves to goals. In fact, we even forget that we forgot.

Attracting Optimum health

If we have a particular illness or complaint, it will take centre stage in our life. We will work to get better. We focus and add effort to achieve the goal. Attracting optimum health could be on our radar—our central planning focus—all the time. It's easy to instigate. Like a commitment to walk daily becomes a habit by constant repetition, so commitment to visualising abundant health or daily yoga, Tai Chi or Qi gong can be. I know I fall into error when I get carried away and I focus on attracting a particular event or set of circumstances. I am healthy and I desire something strongly enough to forget about the little things in life. I forget to work on maintaining my health. Then I get run down, catch a cold, feel miserable and know that

I have forgotten my health again. It is embarrassing being a teacher of health then being sick yourself through neglect.

Using emotions

Emotions are like food colouring in a recipe. They boost anything else you do. A little goes a long way. Visualising a desired outcome is powerful but if you add your emotions to the mix and you feel as if you already have the outcome, suddenly the energy is transformed to super power status. It is sometimes difficult to imagine being well while constant pain seems to say you are not, but getting lost in the feeling of wellness can make the mind forget. It is like being in a game on the computer. Once the game is on the whole screen is taken up and you can't work on your budget spread-sheet at the same time—not that you would want to. The mind can run mutually exclusive dreams and make it all seem like real as much as the computer can on a screen. In fact it can do better than that.

In your mind you can picture the health you have beside a picture of the state of health you would like and create a different ending to your story. You can colour your life differently by using emotions.

Recipe: Colour your life

- Think of your life as it is but imagine it in black and white.
- Think of your life how you would like it to be but imagine that in colour.
- Put both images into the screen of your mind at the same time
- Shrink the black and white picture of reality to the bottom left of your screen, making it the past.
- Make the coloured dream fill the entire screen. Add sounds. Feel the feelings it creates as strongly as you can. Wallow in the beauty and live in that new awesome outcome for as long as you can.

- Hold the vibration of your desire for at least 2 minutes. (Even 20 seconds will make a difference.)
- Repeat often.
- Every time you repeat living the new coloured awesome feeling reality it draws it closer through the UNIVERSAL Law of Attraction.

LIFE IS HOLISTIC

Life is incredible and so are we. We humans are not here just as a body. We have a mind through which we experience this life. We are a spirit within this body that has this mind. We exist on many levels. We have many selves within our own universe. I am a wife, a mother, a writer, a book-keeper, a holiday-maker, a daughter, a gardener, a sister . . . . And the list goes on.

Just as we have many roles on many levels, so the different aspects of our lives are interwoven and connected. Have you noticed that when you have problems in one area of your life they soon spill over? When our business fails, our relationships become tense, finances tumble, and we develop ulcers and feel sick. The opposite is also true. When we fall in love, the whole world takes on a rosy glance. The boss may complain to us and we may have a flat tyre while driving to work, but nothing really gets us down. Nothing upsets us except removal of our happiness. Like when we want to go on a round the world honeymoon and the bank-manager tells us all we can afford is a walk to MacDonald's.

The areas of our life overlap because we are the common denominator. It is all us. My life is me and all the different aspects and characters that make up me. Your life is a reflection of all the thoughts, desires, roles and stories of your life. Our attitudes, thoughts, ideas, and feelings spill over from one area to another. In that way, the techniques we use on self-healing can be adapted to other areas of our lives. We can improve our relationships by meditating, visualising, and using positive affirmations. Finances can improve when we take out some of the negative thoughts and we stop looking at money as evil. Just because some people choose to change and become snobs when they acquire lots of money, does not mean you should not improve your income. Each person has his or her problems, and with the problems come just as individual solutions. If there are problems at work, maybe a change in attitude will smooth out the differences. Maybe, just accepting a colleague as an insensitive twit will help stop being constantly irritated by him or her. Silently sending universal energy and unconditional love to a difficult work-mate may iron out the problem. Our personal life has the ability to improve as we learn and grow. Self-healing is only the first step to a most wonderful journey to knowing the inner you and taking control of your own life. Self-healing is not only the first step but also the most powerful.

TOUCHING YOUR PASSION

When we do what we love, we live in a health-promoting atmosphere. The energy we have around us is positive, full of hope and joy. We touch the vibration of awesomeness and our mind is open to being invincible. Doing what we love produces a natural harmony within body mind and spirit and we feel connected to All-that-is—everything. I have watched an old man sit with crippled fingers at the piano and play the most wonderful music. As he was lost in the experience his fingers glided over the keys and he seemed to lose years. As he finished the smile on his face was wonderful to behold but afterwards the pain in his arthritic fingers brought him back to his reality. In his passion he escaped and experienced wellness.

With self-healing or any positive development just, begin. If there is something that you have always wanted to do, then do it. Taste it. Try it.

I do feel I should stress, however, that one must stay within some limits of common sense. I remember one case—Pat was included in a discussion of the benefits of vegetarianism. The conclusion drawn by the group was that if you truly crave something, then it might be better to have it than to deny for the sake of someone else's beliefs. Pat transferred the wisdom into his own life and returned to his drugs habit thinking it was better to do what he craved than what society, the law and his family wanted. The experiment and resulting habit took him months to recover from.

When you begin something new, there will be the positive vibration of excitement. This early enthusiasm and excitement should create enough energy to keep you going. Healing is a forward moving energy and so is passion for life and living. Doing that which you truly love to do, be it knitting, or driving racing cars, creates positive energy which is beneficial to the healing process. Find your passion, fulfil your dreams, and be healed!

Life's purpose

I know that each of us has come to this life for a purpose. We generally forget what that purpose was when we are born and start learning how to use our body, make sounds and survive in the social environments of family. Some people know from an early age that they are going to be a doctor or ballet dancer and just focus on that. Their dream and purpose are strong and they find ways to make it all happen.

Others of us follow a path and then get knocked and wonder why we are here. Nothing stands out and we live as though we are either a rat on a wheel or we escape into an electronic parallel. We keep up with the real-life shows and have to know what everyone else is doing, follow others' life pattern rather than creating something for ourselves. The happiest people are sometimes those who have descended to the depths of depression and then found where they could help others. They have found a purpose in giving of themselves, their labour, their guidance or their understanding to someone less fortunate. That giving is then rewarded by gratitude and appreciation. Finding a worthwhile purpose in life that leaves a legacy for others is a path to happiness that will flow into health of body, mind and spirit.

We are more than our body and current circumstances. Discovering that, can be your start to finding your divine purpose. As you recognise that you are a magnificent being, in a physical body with a magnificent mind to let you experience wonder and beauty you cannot feel other than awesome. When you touch you infinite personal power, you will realise what an awesome creature you really are and create the life you really want.

Your purpose is to live your life and be all you can be!

Enjoy the challenge of creating that and revel in all the health and happiness that goes with that.

Conclusion

Use from this book what you need and then go beyond.

If you have a health challenge, discover for yourself the magic of vibrational oils and therapeutic massage, try the herbal teas, and incense. Chronic Fatigue Syndrome has been known to be cured by Chinese Herbs and ADD by supplementing the diet with Trace Elements. What cures can you find in aromatherapy, reflexology, homeopathy and acupuncture? Look amid the books, the courses, and the advertisements. Choose and map out a path to healing for yourself. Remember to add some common sense into the mix. When you become in tune with your own healing energies, you will find your particular path. In fact, you will wonder why it has taken you so long to see the obvious. Why it has taken you so long to find your beautiful, vibrantly healthy, happy self.

Wayne Dyer quoted this poem by Samuel Taylor Coleridge in his book *Real Magic.*

> *What if you slept?*
> *And what if,*
> *in your sleep*
> *you dreamed?*
> *And what if,*
> *in your dream*
> *you went to heaven*
> *and there plucked*

a strange and beautiful flower?
And what if,
When you awoke,
you had the flower
in your hand.

This book is my strange flower manifested into the physical.

And my part is fulfilled.
Your part is just beginning!
Enjoy the recipes—
Create **your wonderful life** as **you** dream it . . . .

List of Recipes

Hi-Lo 55
Total Absorption in Fun and Laughter 56
Thoughts and Feelings 57
Discovery...60
Focus on Healing 61
White Light...62
Replacing Lack with Love..64
Sending Love...65
Everyday Affirmation...70
Specific Affirmation 71
New Broom 74
Discover Your Goals...75
Gold Card..76
Norm's recipe 77
Cheat Version 77
My Mates Analysis..78
Change my mates..79
When you—I Feel..80
Common Sense body action steps...82
Complete Breath Standing...83
Complete Breath Sitting...83
Cleansing Breathe...84
Complete Stretch..86
Loosening Up 87
Conscious Relaxation 98

Counting Down 99
Counting Down—deeper session 100
Mantra Method 101
Laying On of your own Hands..102
Laying Hands on Another 103
Feel, See, and Hear.. 106
Cleansing Breath 108
The Rainbow of Life 110
Regeneration..114
Broken Record (Mantra Method) 118
Rating the Problem.. 123
Exterminate Negatives #1—Delete or Cancel................125
Exterminate Negatives #2—Watch it.............................125
Exterminate Negatives #3—The 100% Switch 126
Exterminate Negatives #4—Clown Around.................... 126
Exterminate Negatives #5—The Clear Path 127
Exterminate Negatives #6—Magic Fire......................... 128
Cleansing the Mind.. 129
Thought and Belief Analysis part 1................................132
Thought and Belief Analysis part 2................................133
Decreasing the Negative Power......................................134
Increasing the Positive Power 134
Building New Beliefs...135
Self-talk Watchdog.. 136
Contemplate the Prayer of Serenity 138
Acknowledge your success 138
Love Thy Enemy 141
Apologise...142
Absentee Apology..142
Cleaning Up 143
Write it Out.. 144
The Imaginary Friend 145
Letting Go of Anger... 146
Cry..147
Fight Fire With Fire...147
Laugh it Off..147

Reprogramming your Bio-Computer 149
Lisa's Reprogramming 150
Prayer...............156
Faith in self...............158
Building faith...............162
Practice Dying...............168
Live Today...............171
To Indulge in the moment 174
In God's hands...............180
Making holy water 182
Energising goals...............190
Colour your life...............192

List of Diagrams

Healing Wheel..48
The wheel of life 164

Bibliography

The following reading list includes some of the books and some of the authors, whose work I have read and devoured over the past couple of decades . . .

I recommend any of these texts merely as a starting point for further reading.

Bristol, Claude. The Magic of Believing. Pocket Books. New York. 1948

Diamond, Harvey and Marilyn. Fit for Life. Bantam Books. Toronto. 1987

Dyer, Dr Wayne W. Your Sacred Self. Harper Collins.USA. 1995.

- Real Magic.
- You'll See it When You Believe it
- and many more.

Kehoe, John. Mind Power. Zoetic Inc. Canada. 1994

- A vision of Power and Glory.
- Money, Success and You.

OgMandino The Greatest Miracle in the World Bonanza Books. New York.1981.

- The Greatest Secret in the World

Ostrom, Joseph. You and Your Aura. The Aquarian Press.England. 1987.

Ouseley, S.G.J. The Power of the Rays:The Science of Colour Healing. Wheaton and Co, Exeter. 1951.

Rampa, T. Lobsang. You—Forever. Corgi Books. London. 1965

Robbins, Anthony. Unlimited Power.London.1988.

Wilde, Stuart. Whispering Winds of Change. Nacson& Sons. Sydney. 1993.

- Miracles.
- Affirmations.
- The Secrets of Life
- And many more.

More of the Authors with similar material are:

- Dale Carnegie
- Louise Hay
- Deepac Chopra
- Napoleon Hill
- Shakti Gawain
- U S Anderson
- Tom Hopkins
- Jose Silva
- Emile Coue`

It never hurts to read from The Holy Books :

- The Bible,
- Koran,
- Tao

Topics to search for more information within the healing arts include

- Healing with Colour;
- Healing visualisations;

- Visualisations;
- Essential oils & Aromatherapy
- Healing with Crystals
- Acupuncture
- Ancient Chinese Medicine

Some of the areas of interest that I have pursued (in no particular order) are:

- Auras and Chakras
- The Mind, Self-development and Self-help books
- Psychic Awareness and Spiritualism
- Nutrition, Diet and Supplements
- Fitness, Massage and Yoga
- Psychology
- Native Cultures and Beliefs
- Meditations and Visualisations

Among the many courses and seminars (live and/or on tape) which I can personally recommend:

- Mind Powers and Dynamic Thinking with John Kehoe.
- Michael Rowland's seminars
- I was Born Rich from Bob Proctor
- Real Magic by Wayne Dyer
- Books on the Law of Attraction by Ester & Jerry Hicks
- A Course in Miracles
- Essential Oil training Days and Workshops

The world is out there waiting for you to discover it. When you can tune into yourself and your personal needs, the recipes for good health will jump out from everywhere.

Have fun and enjoy the process . . .

Index

A

Acceptance   31, 50, 57, 102, 137-8
Affirmations   x, 17-18, 50, 67-71, 76,
     193, 206
Attitudes   28-30, 33, 44, 120, 131, 193
Attracting optimum health   191

B

Basic Principles   1

C

Choice   ix, 16-17, 26, 30, 42, 80, 94,
     102, 113, 117, 132, 166, 178
Common fears   122

D

Depression   43, 50, 66, 73, 89, 104,
     150, 181, 195
Diet   ix, 38, 42, 66, 85, 92-3, 124,
     129, 187, 197, 207

Diversity of prayer   154
Dying   3, 7, 51, 56-7, 64, 163, 165-8,
     179

E

Energy   19-25, 55-6, 64-6, 78-9,
     95-6, 101-3, 109-16, 125-6,
     128-9, 138-40, 160-2, 173,
     177-81, 190, 194-5
Energy balance   25, 45, 55, 66
Environment   28, 41-3, 73-4, 78,
     115, 131
Evoking the law of attraction   189
Exterminate negative thoughts   124

F

Faith   49, 51, 77, 101, 112, 155-62,
     182, 184
Faith in a supreme being   160
Faith in your medical practitioner
     159
Faith in yourself as a healer   157

Fears and barriers   120
focusing   5, 12, 14, 20, 31, 38, 43-4,
   49-50, 59-62, 66, 112-13, 118-19,
   138-9, 157, 172
Four Aspects   48-9

G

Games   38, 86, 121, 131, 175
Goal setting   74, 189

H

Healing others   103
Healing with colours   115

J

Jesus Christ   177

L

Letting go   3, 45, 143, 146, 158,
   167,
Life is holistic   193
Life's purpose   195
Living in the moment   173
Love   37-8, 49-50, 63-6, 71, 112,
   141, 144, 150-1, 154-5, 167-8,
   170-1, 176, 182, 193-5,

M

Mental power boosters   52
Mind control   121

N

Natural healing system   9-10
Negative surge   184
Negative thoughts   45, 114, 121,
   123-5, 128-9, 143, 194

O

Obsessive thoughts   127
Oxygen   41, 82-5, 89

P

Persistence   35, 128
Prayer   x, 3, 138, 153-6, 183, 188
Prognosis   3, 5, 16, 159

R

Rebuilding faith   161
Reprogramming the memory   147,
   150
Responsibility   viii-xi, 15-17, 42, 47,
   80, 149

S

Self-talk   61, 136, 200
Source   14, 35, 47, 49, 64-5, 94-6,
   101, 112, 114, 120, 130, 147, 156,
   158, 166-8
Staying fit   85
Stress   ix, 6, 16, 23, 38, 42-4, 73, 82,
   90, 98-9, 104, 109, 112, 121-3,
   147

Stress relievers   90
Stretching for fitness   86

T

Three levels of mind   119
Tools for enhancing your vibration
      181
Touching your passion   194
Transforming beliefs   133

U

Universal energy   19, 96, 101, 162,
      194
Using emotions   192

V

Vibrational healing   159, 179-81
Visualisation   52, 105-6, 109-10,
      114, 127-8, 131, 144, 168, 188,
      190

W

Walking backwards   89
Walking for exercise   88
Walking to lose weight   88
Walking to relieve depression   89
Walking to relieve stress   90
Water   38, 41, 68, 76-7, 82, 91-3,
      95, 101, 112, 114, 120, 128, 140,
      159, 182-3